I dedicate this book to my inspiration of a daughter, Nevaeh.

Thank you for bringing meaning to my life and opening a world I never knew existed.

And to the many single parents and family members that may be adjusting with their children on the spectrum, know that you are strong, capable and wise.

YOU GOT THIS.

Contents

Introduction

When my daughter was diagnosed with autism spectrum disorder in 2006, I had no idea what autism was. I had never even heard the word until then. Slowly, I felt my world drift away, and I cried over the life my daughter would have. I questioned whether I would be able to raise her on my own as a single parent. Nothing alarmed me more than the feeling of uncertainty.

The days went by and I kept thinking, *there's no way my daughter has autism; they don't know what they are talking about.* Just as I got enough nerve to call up the diagnostician and give her a piece of my mind, I received my daughter's comprehensive evaluation.

Words cannot describe the incredible amount of misinformation I was given.

According to the evaluation, my daughter was "severely mentally retarded." And if the shock of those words were not enough, there was no follow-up or recommended course of action. I was left twisting in the wind.

I was discouraged, but I did not let that stop me. I poured over every bit of research I could find. I took to peer-reviewed journals, blogs, and critically acclaimed novels. I called professionals in their field and asked for informational interviews. I sat inside some of the most prestigious libraries I could find and I got to work.

While the information I found was great in supporting my foundational knowledge of ASD, I still felt like I could not relate to what was written as a first-time, single mother. I was not interested in hearing an account from another mother, psychologist or celebrity who had far more resources than I could even imagine at the time.

I did not see *me* on paper.

At the time, I had very little money; trust in myself, information and support. I needed to know someone like me could make.

During the writing process, I was not prepared for the tears that came as I memories I had hoped to forget pushed their way to the surface. I wrestled a lot with putting a portion of my story on paper.

Exposing myself and acknowledging my own shortcomings took an incredible amount of strength with just the right amount of crazy sprinkled on top. While I recognize this is my story of becoming who I am as a woman and a parent, I am well aware that I share my truth with my daughter's life and experiences. I spoke, at length, with Nevaeh about whether I should write this book. Nevaeh's response was:

*Mom, yes. I think a lot of moms should learn from you. You make this look easy and you always smile and look so good doing it. I also wanted people to know that just because you have autism doesn't mean you **are** autism.*

My daughter is a lion.

I traded my entire 20s to see the growth in my daughter. To fight with doctors, struggle with schools and compete with the media that continually attacked special education children. I pushed myself in every direction so that I could be the mother I instinctively imagined I could be.

The fight has been a long road of perseverance and self-discovery. And although my battle wounds run deep, I would do it again if it meant seeing my baby hit every milestone and slice through every doctor's report shouting, "victory!"

I wrote this book not in chronological order, but in pockets of moments I felt made more of an impact and would be what you needed to hear.

Over the next few pages, I will hit you with facts on facts on facts. My language will shift from a formal research-driven tone, to that of your best friend who will binge watch Netflix with you.

My goal is to share very personal and crucial moments of my life as I believe this will prepare you for the new world you now find yourself in.

Proceed with caution.

If you are not trying to be encouraged, lifted, reminded to do and be better, learn about the brain or do some serious soul searching, you might want to leave this book alone.

I make no excuses, so I accept none.

Everything you have ever needed has been placed inside of you. You just need a little help focusing inward to pull that gift out. Put on your boxing gloves. Together, we can do this.

The Structure of the Human Brain

The brain is a fabulously complicated organ that regulates functions of our body, interprets information from the world, and embodies the essence of who we are as people. The brain is the gateway of our ideas, memory, speech, and the performance of our movements.

It is necessary to have a working knowledge of our brain and its functioning to understand what may be going on in the minds of children with Autism Spectrum Disorder (ASD). Welcome to my Brain Anatomy and Physiology Class. Feel free to take notes; there will be a test.

The brain is divided into three categories, the **hindbrain**, **midbrain**, and **forebrain**.

The **hindbrain** is composed of the medulla, the pons, and the cerebellum. The hindbrain coordinates functions that are key to survival, like our reflex action, respiratory rhythm, motor activity, sleep, and wakefulness. (Kalat, 2016).

The **midbrain** serves crucial functions in motor movement, particularly movements of the eye, and in auditory and visual processing. The **forebrain** contains the entire cerebrum and several structures directly nestled within it - the thalamus, hypothalamus, the pineal gland, and the limbic system.

Let's take a closer look at the cerebrum of the forebrain.

When you picture the iconic shape of the human brain, the majority of what's visible is the cerebrum with its wrinkly, pinkish-grey outer appearance.

The cerebrum is the most highly developed part of the human brain and is responsible for thinking, perceiving, producing and understanding life around us. The outer layer of the cerebrum is called the cerebral cortex.

If you have watched the X-Men movies or comics published by Marvel Comics, you might have remembered Professor Charles Xavier using Cerebro, a fictional device to find other mutants by their brain activity. The idea of Cerebro enhancing Professor X's ability might not be too off from the operation of our cerebrum and cerebral cortex.

Most information processing occurs in the cerebral cortex which is divided into four lobes have a specific function.

These lobes are the frontal lobe, parietal lobe, temporal lobe, and occipital lobe.

Although we now understand that most brain functions rely on several different regions across the entire brain working together, each lobe bears the bulk of certain functions. (Queensland University, 2018).

The frontal lobe is important for cognitive functions and control of voluntary movement or activity.
The parietal lobe processes information about temperature, taste, touch and movement, while the occipital lobe is primarily responsible for vision.

The temporal lobe processes memories, integrating them with sensations of taste, sound, sight and touch.

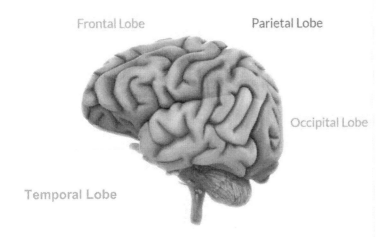

Figure 1 Locations of the temporal lobe, frontal lobe, parietal lobe, and occipital lobe.

As mentioned, the brain is a fabulously complicated organ with so much planning like a woven tapestry of neurons that design who we are. Having working knowledge of the brain will allow you to understand when you hear information about your children with ASD. There is always a reason behind a certain set of actions.

What is Autism Spectrum Disorder?

ASD refers to a multi-layered **neurodevelopmental disorder** characterized by persistent barriers in communication and social interactions along with, repetitive patterns of behavior, interests or activities.

Most people have a hard time defining ASD because no two people are alike. What works for one may not work for another. What impacts one may not impact another. In essence, ASD is the equivalent of requiring a made-to-measure bespoke suit in life.

People with ASD are referred to as being "on the spectrum" which refers to the broad range of symptoms, skills, and levels of functioning that can occur in people with ASD from mild to severe.

A person on the severe side of ASD usually is nonverbal and lacks coordination. This person is also on the alternative curriculum at school and needs more assistance in their everyday lives including tasks like getting dressed and brushing teeth.

A person on the mild end of the spectrum is usually verbal and can access the core curriculum at school. This person has executive functioning skills and is able to prepare dress themselves as well as taking care of other hygiene tasks themselves daily.

The American Psychiatric Association (APA) has created a guide called the Diagnostic and Statistical Manual of Mental Disorders (DSM-5), which is used by practitioners to diagnose and define mental health disorders.

The DSM-5 is the product of more than 10 years of effort by hundreds of international mental health professionals.

According to the DSM-5, Dr. Cecil R. Reynold and Dr. Randy W. Kamphaus conclude there are three severity levels of ASD that is broken up in three different severity levels.

Severity Level 3 Social communication	"Requiring very substantial support" Restricted, repetitive behaviors
Severe deficits in verbal and nonverbal social communication skills cause severe impairments in functioning, very limited initiation of social interactions	Inflexibility of behavior, extreme difficulty coping with change, or other restricted/ repetitive behaviors markedly interfere with functioning in all spheres. Great distress/ difficulty changing focus or action.
Severity Level 2 Social communication	"Requiring substantial support" Restricted, repetitive behaviors
Marked deficits in verbal and nonverbal social communication skills; social impairments apparent even with supports in place; limited initiation of social interactions	Inflexibility of behavior, difficulty coping with change, or other restricted/ repetitive behaviors appear frequently enough to be obvious to the casual observer and interfere with functioning in a variety of contexts. Distress and/ or difficulty changing focus or action.
Severity Level 1 Social communication	"Requiring support" Restricted, repetitive behaviors
Without supports in place, deficits in social communication cause noticeable impairments. May appear to have decreased interest in social interactions.	Inflexibility of behavior causes significant interference with functioning in one or more contexts. Difficulty switching between activities

I recommend you take the time to read the DSM-5 in its entirety when you are getting your children evaluated or reevaluated.

Since you now know autism is a **neurodevelopmental disorder**, let's unpack the word neurodevelopmental. The word "neuro" refers to nerves and nervous system. The word "develop" means to *bring out the possibilities*. When you put "neurodevelopmental" together, it means the nerves interchange differently and react individually—**a new way to bring out possibilities of the mind.**

Things that may come easily to you – like holding a conversation, understanding your surroundings or being able to maintain eye contact with someone – are more challenging for persons with autism spectrum disorder. Not because someone with ASD lacks the ability or potential, but because the mind operates on a different level and plays by a separate set of rules.

Now let's get ready to use what you learned from the Structure of the Human Brain.

Brain development during early childhood in ASD seems to be predominated by an enlarged brain volume of the **frontal** and **temporal lobes** followed by arrested growth and a possible declined volumetric capacity of the brain after 10-15 years of age. (Kim, Cho, et al, 2017).

For example, abnormalities in the frontal lobe are related to deficits in social language processing and social attention. Adnormailities in the the **parietal lobe**, and amygdala explains impairments of social behaviors. Most tests conclude that many people with ASD carry these same distinctions within the mind.

This means that the normal makeup of a person with ASD is entirely different as it relates to the social and communication concerns.

A brain-tissue article in *Neuron* from the Columbia University Medical Center (CUMCR) suggests that children with ASD have a surplus of **synapses**. According to David Sulzer, professor of neurobiology at CUMCR, the study is the "first time that anyone has looked for, and seen, a **lack of pruning** during development of children with autism."

The way our brains process is such a unique and intricately designed from of operations. The pruning process is our brain's proper system of checks and balances.

When our brains do not **prune properly**, during adolescence, there is an excess of **synapses**.

What are synapses?

Imagine jumping across a puddle of water on your walk home. A synapse is similar to that, but instead of you jumping from one dry area to another, information jumps from one brain cell to another. More specifically, synapses are the junction where neurons connect and transmits information to the rest of our body.

What is the pruning process?

Think about gardening. If you want your plants to blossom, you have to use your green thumb and remove bits of the plant at a time. Doing so allows the plant to flourish.

In the brain, the pruning process reduces the number of brain cells and synapses as your brain develops. When you were a baby, a burst of synapse formation prepared your brain for all the information you would learn. Pruning eliminates the extra half of these cortical synapses by late adolescence because they are no longer needed.

To sum it all up, the study suggests that information in the mind of a child is firing at lightning speed. But in the mind of a child with ASD, information might be misconstrued or processed faster than what we think. (Dawson, 2008)

When my daughter was a little girl, maintaining eye contact was very hard for her. Nevaeh would look away or down after being introduced to someone. While most people find that behavior rude or dismissive, I found that Nevaeh paid so much attention to the details in a person's face within a split second.
It was as if her brilliant mind had catalogued over 100 images of that person and mostly likely knew the curves of their faces better than they did. As you can imagine, this is a lot of information to process.

So, while folks thought Nevaeh was being antisocial,

I knew that when Nevaeh looked away, she was essentially resetting her mind.

A study from Stanford University School of Medicine that was published in the journal, *Brain*, compared brain scans from children with autism and typically developing children. The study focused on the pathway in the brain that usually makes social interactions feel rewarding. They found that nerve-fiber fields along this pathway were less dense in the brains of the children who had autism.

These structural differences suggest that social interaction might be inherently less rewarding for people with autism, which could interfere with the development of complex social skills.

For the typical individual, communicating and getting things off your chest is satisfying. We all want to be acknowledged and heard. But Stanford's finding suggests that our ASD kiddos might not place much interest on it because it's less rewarding to share for them and more rewarding to understand information in its simplistic form.

Dr. Helen Tager-Flusberg, Director of the Center for Autism Research Excellence at Boston University, has conducted brain imaging studies on children and adults with autism, between age 4 and 24 year.

Similar to Stanford's testing, Dr. Tager-Fulsberg's finding suggests there is a degree of reduced asymmetry within the brain. After further investigation, she concluded, "we have examined the thickness of cortical areas. We found that in the right hemisphere, the areas associated with social functioning and imitation – part of the so-called "mirror neuron system" – have reduced the thickness and that this reduction is also related to the severity of social symptoms in ASD."

Have you ever had a conversation with a friend who was angry about a situation and the more they shared their story with you, the angrier you got for them? That is the mirror neuron effect. Mirror neurons are cells that are active during movement and while watching someone else perform the same movements. (Rizzolatti & Sinigaglia, 2010).

Let's unpack the biological psychology a step further.

ASD is a neurodevelopmental disorder which means, the mind of a person with ASD processes, interrupts, responds and accepts information differently than those who do not have ASD. Not only that, it is less rewarding to verbally communicate and socialize than it is for the typical person.

The studies suggest that a person with ASD finds comfort from understanding the logic in a situation rather than staying in the shadows of nuance.

Some facts about autism:

- The Centers for Disease Control and Prevention (CDC) estimates autism's prevalence as 1 in 68 children in the United States.
    - This includes 1 in 42 boys and 1 in 189 girls.
- Around one-third of people with autism remain nonverbal.
- Around one-third of people with autism have an intellectual disability.
- Certain medical and mental health issues frequently accompany autism. They include:
    - gastrointestinal (GI) disorders

- seizures
- sleep disturbances
- attention deficit and hyperactivity disorder (ADHD)
- anxiety
- phobias

Now, for parents who happened across this book and are wondering if their children may be on the spectrum, here are some things to look out for.

What are some common signs of ASD?

Typically developing infants are social by nature. They gaze at faces, turn toward voices, grasp a finger, and even smile by 2 to 3 months of age.

By contrast, most children who develop autism have difficulty engaging in the give-and-take of everyday human interactions.

By 8 to 10 months of age, many infants do not respond to their names and show a reduced interest in people.

As toddlers, many children with autism have challenges in playing games with other toddlers, do not mimic the actions of others and appear to prefer to play alone.

In other cases, children may develop ordinarily until the second or even third year of life, but then start to withdraw and become indifferent to social engagement.

Social impairment and communication difficulties.

Some children with ASD may have delayed speech and language skills, may repeat phrases, and give unrelated answers to questions. Also, people with ASD can have a hard time using and understanding non-verbal cues such as gestures, body language, or tone of voice.

Social interactions are a hard thing to master as an adult. Nuance is extremely hard to understand for children who do not yet have that area developed in their brain. As you have read, about the structure of the brain, the part that controls executive functioning like impulse control and emotional regulation has not even been formed it until after adolescents.

Encourage your child to start small. Before you enter a new space, tell your child to find one person and simply smile at them *if* they like something about them.

For example, I encouraged my daughter to ask servers at restaurants about their favorite dishes, which helped Nevaeh to order on her own. This led to Nevaeh happily engaging with whoever crossed her path.

As long as you keep your baby involved and steadily nudge them a little farther out of their comfort zone, you will see a marvelous change.

ASD Self-Check

This self-test was adapted from the modified checklist for autism in toddlers (m-chat-r) as well as the childhood autism spectrum test from the University of Cambridge. The test is designed to screen for the possibility of ASD in children.

Q. 1 If you point at something across the room, does your child look at it?

    ○ Yes

    ○ No

Q. 2 Have you ever wondered if your child might be hearing impaired?

    ○ Yes

    ○ No

Q. 3 Does your child make unusual finger movements near their eyes?

    ○ Yes

    ○ No

Q. 4 Does your child get upset by everyday noises?

    ○ Yes

    ○ No

Q. 5 Does your child appear to notice unusual details that others miss?

- ○ Yes
- ○ No

Q. 6 Does your child like to do things over and over again, in the same way all the time?

- ○ Yes
- ○ No

Q. 7 Does your child have an interest that takes up so much time that they do little else?

- ○ Yes
- ○ No

Q. 8 Does your child have difficulty understanding the rules for polite behavior?

- ○ Yes
- ○ No

Q. 9 Does your child appear to have an unusual memory for details?

- ○ Yes
- ○ No

Q. 10 If something new happens, does your child look at your face to see how you feel about it?

- ○ Yes
- ○ No

Q. 11 Does your child understand when you tell them to do something?

○ Yes

○ No

Q. 12 Does your child try to get you to watch them?

○ Yes

○ No

Q. 13 If you turn your head to look at something, does your child look around to see what you are looking at?

○ Yes

○ No

Q. 14 Does your child try to copy what you do?

○ Yes

○ No

Q. 15 Does your child look you in the eye when you are talking to them, playing with them, or dressing them?

○ Yes

○ No

Q. 16 When you smile at your child, do they smile back at you?

○ Yes

○ No

Q. 17 Does your child respond when you call their name?

○ Yes

○ No

Q. 18 Does your child show you things by bringing them to you or holding them up for you to see—not to get help, but just to share?

○ Yes

○ No

Q. 19 Is your child interested in other children?

○ Yes

○ No

Q. 20 Does your child point with one finger to show you something interesting?

○ Yes

○ No

Q. 21 Does your child point with one finger to ask for something or to get help?

○ Yes

○ No

Q. 22 Does your child like climbing on things?

○ Yes

○ No

Q. 23 Does your child play pretend or make-believe?

○ Yes

○ No

Q. 24 Does your child like to be bounced?

○ Yes

○ No

Q. 25 Does your child join in playing games with other children easily?

○ Yes

○ No

Q. 26 Does your child come up to you spontaneously for a chat?

○ Yes

○ No

Q. 27 Was your child speaking by the age of two?

○ Yes

○ No

Q. 28 Does your child enjoy playing sports?

○ Yes

○ No

Q. 29 Is it important to your child to fit in with their peer group?

○ Yes

○ No

Q. 30 Can your child keep a two-way conversation going?

○ Yes

○ No

Answer Key:

If you have answered **NO** to questions:

1, 3, 8, and 10-30

And, **YES** to questions:

2, 4, 5, 6, 7, and 9

I urge you to contact your healthcare provider and get an official evaluation completed. You may also go to a diagnostic center in your city for an independent evaluation if you are unable to receive a referral from your physician.

A detailed assessment requires a multidisciplinary team, including a psychologist, neurologist, psychiatrist, speech therapist, and other professionals who diagnose and treat children with ASD.

Although I am not a physician, in addition to understanding the above information, I suggest you pay attention to your child's hearing and tongue movements. You may want to get your child's hearing tested to make sure there are no impairments. is no make sure your child isn't suffering from low volume or blockage getting your child's hearing tested along with make sure there isn't additional tissue restricting movement of your child's tongue.

To my parents who have already received their diagnosis, please take a moment to review the questions above and make notes.

I would like for you to jot down when you noticed a behavior in your child to better help you reference when speak to any professionals in reference to your child.

_____

_____

_____

If you have yet to make changes or adjust to best support your child, here is your time.

Whatever thought you have, whatever promise you can make for yourself and your children, please take the time to write that down on the line below:

_____

_____

_____

_____

My child will be able to:

_____

_____

_____

I believe:

_____

_____

_____

I can:

_____

Now, after all my research and pouring over information, creating journals that look like the manic scribbles of a mad man, I deduce that: *A person with Autism Spectrum Disorder (ASD) has a neurodevelopmental intricacy, requiring modified forms of instruction for new possibilities of the mind to develop.* Perhaps an expression of a thoughtful and linear superpower.

However, the expression of a superpower is not to be confused with the misrepresentation that all children with ASD have some sort of genius – a ridiculous expectation that further adds to the many myths of ASD.

Contrary to popular believe, being autistic does not automatically mean your child will solve the world's wonders.

The expectation of genius, or having Savant syndrome, places an incredible burden for these young people to "perform". Savant syndrome is a rare extraordinary, condition in which persons with serious mental disabilities, including autistic disorder, have some 'island of genius' which stands in marked, incongruous contrast to overall handicap.

Savant syndrome, with its 'islands of genius', has a long history. In Rimland's survey of 5400 children with autism, 531 were reported by parents to have special abilities. According to the survey, 10% incidence of savant syndrome has become the generally accepted figure in autistic disorder.

While having Savant syndrome along with autism spectrum disorder is unlikely, there is evidence to suggest that children with ASD often portray signs of excellence and above average intelligence (Levy, 2003).

Our little superheroes can have astounding focus and recite to you the entire genealogy of a dinosaur, the anatomical makings of the heart, an entire movie front to back or make you feel deeply in ways you have never known. Our kids are capable of extraordinary feats, but we should rest in the fact that they being who they are is a miracle within itself.

It is very possible for all of us to be both a work in progress and a masterpiece.

Our Credo of Understanding

First things, first—take all the misnomers and misrepresentation of autism and pack it into a tiny box, and never open it again. This is your clean slate, a blank canvas. Your life is the most exceptional work of art ever imagined and from this moment on, you will have real knowledge to guide and your instinct to drive you.

Take a deep breath.

I want you to feel the burdens of doubt lifting off your shoulders. With each of these words you read, I want you to slowly begin to sit up a little taller.

Will your strength to come.

Breathe in. Hold that air. And exhale out.

Trust me. Trust this Process.

Breathe in. Hold that air. And exhale out slowly.

You are perfect.

You are powerful.

You have so much to offer. You are without blame.

Now, get ready for this.

For the autism mom, please know there is nothing you could have done differently to prevent it. You took your prenatal pills. You avoided sushi, alcohol, fumes, chemicals, and dyes for nine months.

You sacrificed and molded into the protective mother you are today.

You did the Heisman on strangers trying to rub your belly, took a few more steps a day, and tried to keep the cravings down.

You were a champion.

You decorated the nursery or special baby spot like a pro and delivered a beautiful child like a hero.

This same sentiment applies if you adopted, had a surrogate, used IVF, or went any other non-traditional route. However, your child came to be with you, you are now their advocate. You did nothing wrong.

In your quiet time, and as you reflect; only you know the specific amount of energy and time you took in all of your research and your vetting processes.

Sometimes we need to sit back and remind ourselves is that **we did nothing wrong.**

As women, we often blame ourselves (especially as single parents), and we do this because everything in our homes, jobs, and relationships inevitably end up becoming our ultimate burden.

We are our own worst critics.

The acknowledgment of taking the blame of autism off your shoulders is as vital as breathing. You are not allowed to feel shame.

The truth of the matter is, if physicians, therapists, psychiatrists, research analysts, and other experts have yet to pinpoint the cause of autism how can you possibly blame yourself?

Finding balance is understanding that the beauty of life is, the process of living. To live is to grow is to stretch is to move in ways uncomfortable or even hurtful. It is the ripping apart of muscle fibers and tendons so that they grow back leaner and stronger and more capable.

Criticism is a luxury you cannot afford. Your bank can't cash it. Your card will not accept it. Your wealth comes in the miracle of a child you now have the gift to parent, love, and mold.

You can do this.

Diagnosis Day

I remember walking into the diagnostic center in my area and feeling like *something* was about to happen. An inexplicable feeling of anxiety overwhelmed me. I felt my heart beating out of tune, and I was unable to catch my breath entirely.

I could not pinpoint why.

There was no particular reason, honestly. Everyone in the diagnostic center spoke to me was very kind. Information was easily accessible and I was offered a cup of water. But somewhere, in the recesses of my mind, I knew my life would never be the same.

Nevaeh and I sat comfortably in our chairs as the psychologist stepped forward to introduce herself. We were then shown to a small room. I remember how the psychologist kept complimenting Nevaeh on how beautiful she was and how her outfit was, "oh, so nice." With each compliment the psychologist gave, I walked a little taller. I knew how to style some hair.

We began with a series of tests where Nevaeh's task was to recognize patterns. The psychologist laid cards out in front of us and was asked to recognize the pattern. .

Next up were Dynamic Indicators of Basic Early Literacy Skills® (**DIBELS**). DIBELS are a set of procedures and measures for assessing the acquisition of early literacy skills. They are designed to be short (one minute) fluency test used to regularly monitor the development of early literacy and early reading skills.

The next test was a combination of colors and then imaginative play. The psychologist laid a few dolls on the table with no instruction and made a "tsk" sound as Nevaeh peered at the dolls and then away with little interest. *This is stupid, Nevaeh never plays with dolls,* I thought to myself. *She's always preferred Legos and puzzles. If you bring some puzzles in here, she'll build you a whole bridge, car, house—you name it.*

The psychologist left the room. I reached into my purse and gave Nevaeh a juice box and asked how she was doing. Nevaeh gave me a look like she was absolutely done with these tests. I giggled, kissed her and said, 'hang in there, kiddo. You're doing great."

And while I moved to reassure Nevaeh, the same feeling of uncertainty crept on my shoulders and hovered like a cloud. I smiled at Nevaeh and felt like a liar. A fraud. I wanted to be a pillar of support for Nevaeh to make it through these tests, but in my heart of hearts, I knew our lives would never be the same.

When the psychologist came back, I noticed her stern expression. Gone was the complimentary and friendly person I had met before, and in their place was a stoic diagnostician.

The psychologist said, quite matter-of-factly, "Ms. Banks, your daughter is autistic." I stopped for a minute and chewed feverishly on the snack I had hidden in my purse. And I laughed incredulously. My laughter had the type of ring to it that was harsh and forced that did nothing but make everyone uncomfortable.

I blinked slowly and said, "I know 'she's *artistic*, my entire family is creative, but why 'isn't she speaking? Why 'isn't she engaging with me? Did we come all this way and spend all this time, JUST for you to tell me she's *artistic*?"

"No, Ms. Banks. I said **'autistic'** not *'artistic.'* She went on to say, "this means she is severely mentally retarded and we will need to work to make her comfortable."

I dropped my Snickers bar and sat dazed as she went down the list of Nevaeh's impairments.

She continued, "Ms. Banks, it is unlikely Nevaeh will live a normal life."

I looked at my daughter who looked at the psychologist and then back down out the floor. She looked defeated. And I felt as though I failed her.

"Ms. Banks? Ms. Banks. Mentally retardation is serious and I want to help you. We should talk about options."

I held my hand up and whispered, "Enough."

I scooped my daughter up, burst through the door and down the hallway. I could hear the psychologist calling my name as I squeezed Nevaeh, held her close to my heart, and ran with her in my arms.

I kept whispering, "You're perfect, baby. You are perfect."

I'm not sure how I drove home, but all of a sudden, there I was. My twin sister Nicole walked silently to my car, got Nevaeh, and walked her into the house. I watched them go as I gripped the steering wheel. When they were gone, I gritted my teeth and hit the steering wheel over and over. I yelled and cried until my voice was gone.

Could I do any of this? Could I do this alone? What type of life was Nevaeh supposed to have?!

When I could not cry anymore, I slowly walked into the house and collapsed on the bed next to my sleeping baby. I looked at her, gathered her in my arms and hugged her as I drifted off to sleep.

The next day, I dragged myself out of bed, stumbled across the wooden floor and into the bathroom. I looked at my swollen eyes in the mirror and traced every curve of my face willing my power to come back.

I took a deep breath and picked up the phone to dial my daughter's father. After the first ring I quickly hung it up and shook my head. He would not have any answers; in fact, he would most likely have more questions or figure out a way to blame me.

I needed a plan first.

I ran the water and watched it go down the drain. Something about watching the water flow into a place never to be seen again made me pull myself back into myself. I splashed water on my face, looked in the mirror, and said, "you ain't no punk."

I dove across the bedroom, opened up my laptop with lightning speed, and began my research. My studies brought me to how our brains function and why. I learned about the specific physiological makeup of our minds and how that shapes our language and behavior. I learned that mental retardation was something entirely different than autism, and since the diagnostician used those words, I felt I could not trust her diagnosis.

Over the next few weeks and months and then years, any research I could get my hands on, I studied. I dissected everything from peer-reviewed journals to crazy pseudo-science articles, color psychology, and cognitive therapy. I felt like a mad scientist, in a cloud of scientific facts along with behavioral analyses. I literally would make breakfast with my left hand and hold my research in my right hand.

Here's a secret, the type of tests to qualify our children for autism do not account for creativity or value diversity. Instead, the tests create stress and provide an amazingly profound artificial environment without giving any feedback on how to achieve better. This equation does not make it any better for our children, us as parents or even the doctors themselves.

Essentially, once a diagnosis has been given, we are either providing our kiddos the best possible chance for mediocrity or the foundation for stern success.

A doctor's best option, in this case, is to offer you a theory that is relative to a tiny moment of observation between the doctor and your child. This short moment does not hold a candle to the instincts you were born with. When all the information points to a 'no,' you can turn it into a 'yes.'

My question to you is, what will you accept? Will you roll over and bury yourself in shades of sorrow, or can you dig deeper and discover what you're made of?

My advice, as a mommy with tenure, is to take the reports under advisement and keep it moving. You will be surprised how well-equipped you are to find the answers. Trust yourself. Be honest with yourself. And most of all, respect the process.

Grief

After my daughter's diagnosis, I experienced a sort of disconnect similar to a complex mix of physical, emotional, and behavioral changes that happens after giving birth. I left like I was in a cloud. I went through the daily motions brilliantly without missing the mark. But I believe my head wasn't entirely in the game.

Even though I was able to move forward and work through setbacks, I still wanted to understand where my tears came from after receiving the full psychological evaluation on my daughter. I had my research, and logically, I was prepared. So why was I sad?

After years of advocacy, years of research, years of grappling with my emotions, I never stopped to realize I went through a process of grieving my daughter, as obscure as that sounds. Perhaps, a better way of describing my grief would be the life I envisioned for my daughter died the minute I received her diagnosis.

Follow me.

As a young mom still finding out about myself, I thought I had it figured out for my newborn. I spent so much time those first few months, nursing and rocking Nevaeh, singing to her and praying for her.

In those late nights, while the world slept, I looked at her perfect fingers and toes and imagined her as a teenager. I mapped out the schools she would enroll in, all the camps she would attend and this big beautiful world she would see. Nevaeh would finish college, marry the man of her dreams, have a fantastic career, and would give me beautiful grandbabies.

This heart of mine, filled with this newfound ability to nurture and protect a child, had no idea what was in store when the doctor first diagnosed her with autism. The love that I had was unchanging; I was so grateful to hold her and kiss her, but at the same time, I was in shock.

Had I known about it then or recognized that my feelings were equally as crucial to the fight of autism, I would have considered going to grief counseling. And, I hope you will consider therapy.

There is nothing wrong in seeking help should you need it. Asking for help is one of the most courageous things you can do.

I kept my grief to myself. I felt like for everyone, especially my friends and family, I had to put up this front to roll with the punches. I felt like I could not give another person anything else to judge me on or gossip over. So, my response to those who asked if I was okay was, "Sure. I've got this handled."

This was a pain I was not used to feeling because I wanted so much for my daughter and I carried that weight with me which is why I can confidently tell you not to carry that burden alone.

The five stages of grief consist of Denial, Anger, Bargaining, Depression, and Acceptance with no clear start or end to any of those moments. The steps of denial are not linear, but more fluid by co-existing or replacing one another in the same space.

No matter how much I love and accept my daughter, there are still very real, very human, fierce emotions that I feel, as her mother. And these emotions have often perfectly been illustrated in how grief and loss are processed in general.

Denial

Here is a truth bomb: everyone around me knew Nevaeh was not a typical child. They knew it. They whispered about it and shunned us for it. And somewhere in my heart, I knew it too. But I still clung to an idea that maybe everyone had gotten it wrong.

Even a year after Nevaeh's diagnosis, I questioned it. After every Individualized Education Plan (IEP) meeting and as Nevaeh crushed every milestone, I questioned it.

What did not help were close ones who would call me with some new evidence to prove Nevaeh did not have autism. Their unassuming hope fueled the fire of denial.

Denial is hard because as mothers, it is almost instinctual to see the good in our children in order to best protect and provide for them. Often, we have blinders on to real issues in our children because to see fault is almost counterintuitive. It is important to not buy into the agenda of viewing our children as disease ridden in need of a cure.

Our children with ASD view the world in such a beautiful way that the untrained eye will never see or experience.

Anger

My anger came from everyone and everything. I would be angry at my daughter's father for not understanding. I would be angry at the kids at the park who did not want to play with her. I was angry at my twin sister for thinking I was making an excuse not to hang when I was unusually tired after a long IEP meeting. I was angry at random people in the grocery store who would stop and stare when Nevaeh screamed from noises that used to startle and hurt her.

I would be angry when Nevaeh locked in on anime or her favorite show and wanted to talk for hours about it. I was angry at myself for not being able to do it all.

So, I think it is fair to say I was randomly and sporadically angry.

I would find myself bothered by little things that would pile up. Eventually, I would reach a boiling point.

I believe the most important role that fueled my anger was because I had this incredible gift of a daughter that I felt I needed to prove to others just how amazing she was.

Bargaining

We all bargain, as parents. We say things, like, "Okay, if you clean your room, we will get pizza." "If you get all A's, I'll buy you a new Nintendo Switch Game." Some people think this is simply enforcing a reward system, but no-it's bargaining. And we all bargain to literally survive as parents.

Bargaining for the autism mom usually goes along with unreasonable expectations.

I was always on the search to find Nevaeh the best occupational therapist, the best school. In my denial of the diagnosis, I would say to myself, "Okay, if I can just find the perfect school with the perfect teacher and the perfect peer group, this new world I'm immersed in would all go away." My denial often gave way for the idea of bargaining. I rarely experienced one without the other.

Eventually I learned that Nevaeh was so incredible that it did not matter where she landed and with whom. Nevaeh could shape the environment to exactly what it needed to be for her and with me at her side, we were unstoppable.

Depression

Research from Harvard Health Publishing suggests that depression does not spring from having too much or too little of certain brain chemicals.

Instead, there are many possible causes of depression, including impaired mood regulation by the brain, genetic vulnerability, stressful life events, medications, and medical problems. It is believed that several of these forces interact to bring on depression (Harvard, 2016).

I used to feel like I had an impenetrable force field around my head. After the needs of my daughter were met, I wanted to climb into bed and wrap the covers around me to sleep my thoughts and feelings away. I felt like I had nothing to give myself after I had given everything I have and then more to my daughter. Soon, I realized that Nevaeh deserved a thriving mother instead of a blanket blob.

I could start small to gain long-term results.

I decided to make my bed every day so I would not crawl back in it. Every time I looked at my made bed, I started to feel satisfied that I accomplished one task outside of being a caregiver. That one task of making my bed inspired me to see what else could be a small gain.

Keeping lists of things I need to accomplish for myself along with what needed to be done for Nevaeh and at work helped to reshape my thinking. And what was even better I began to feel better as I completed and crossed each task off my list.

Most of us feel sad, lonely, or depressed at times. It's a normal reaction to loss, life's struggles, or our own battles with insecurity. But when these feelings become overwhelming, cause physical symptoms, and last for long periods of time, they can keep you from leading a normal, active life.

That's when it's time to seek medical help.

Our life is a marathon life we lead, and there is nothing wrong with reaching out for medical advisement and support.

Acceptance

I reached this stage six years ago. There are key moments when I think back to a time when Nevaeh was on the severe side of the spectrum and I am grateful that we have worked so hard for her to be where she is now, on the opposite side Nevaeh has the biggest heart I have ever seen. Moments when I see her helping another person, coaching, showing empathy, and being firm about her resiliency are the moments I live for.

I discovered quickly that if someone's behavior was not affecting my daughter, why would I hold it personally? If Nevaeh was okay about things, then I needed to learn to accept the life we were given and let the moments that were distracting from our forward progression go.

And the best part? Acceptance brought hope. And Hope is *Better than a Diagnosis*.

Keeping the Faith

I would hold my daughter as she drifted to sleep, speaking words of promise and affirmation over her life. I was thankful for the words she had yet to speak. I believed in my heart that as she grew older, others would listen under her words of wisdom and commanding spirit. I called the leader in her to take form and would whisper, "I see what they do not see. I see you. And I will fight for you."

At church one Sunday, my pastor, Bishop Charles E. Blake said, "If what you see is not what you saw, then what you see is only temporary." That was an incredibly profound statement which helped to reaffirm my radical parenting style. Because what I saw was my daughter living her best life, thriving, and diagnosis, or not, I was going to make sure she could.

I believe one of the most fascinating things about our bodies is our brain and the intricate wiring of our nervous system.

Nowhere in the body is electrical activity better documented than the brain, which contains roughly a hundred electrochemically conductive, biological wires.

It's like a symphony of is flickering with expectation within our bodies.

Our cells are leaping with light. Our bodies are conductors of light. We built to be the light through any dark trail based on the potential written inside our DNA.
My faith in the belief that God would power me through my darkest moments prepared me to become the mother I am today.

I trusted God in all of my decisions. I felt if I had been given this wonderful blessing of a daughter, it meant I had what it took for her to thrive. I did not need anyone's validation. I was born with a seal of validation on me.

When I doubted whether I was strong enough, *I survived.*

When I did not have a roof over my head, *I survived.*

When I went hungry so my daughter could eat, *I survived.*

When I questioned if I was smart enough, *I survived.*

When I did not have anyone to depend on, *I survived.*

How? Because I clung onto the vision and I would not let it go until it came to pass.

Faith requires work. And the minute you accept you'll have to work for everything you want, comes a divine, instinctual instruction of wisdom, guidance and understanding.

Through it all, we have to respect that everything we have ever gone through in life, the heartache, the betrayal, and the sadness--everything was a process to prepare us for the fight of our life.

Stay faithful. Stay committed.

Congratulations on being a survivor. You now have a secret stash of strength for you to tap into when the well runs dry.

The First Time My Daughter Spoke

Figure 2 Nevaeh at her 4th birthday party

"...the best possible way to prepare for tomorrow is to concentrate with all your intelligence, all your enthusiasm, on doing today's work superbly today. That is the only possible way you can prepare for the future." – Dale Carnegie

My daughter was four, and I had not heard the sound of her voice. Sure, Nevaeh cried like most babies, but outside of that she never made one peep.

I longed to hear the tone of her voice and listen to it carry around the room. I drove up and down the coast of California trying therapy centers and speech techniques.

Driving to different therapy places was rough. Nevaeh and I would check into small hotels that I could afford and plan our next place to visit. As we drove from one therapy place to the next, I remember chanting silently, *Antoinette, you are doing the right thing.*

I looked into the rearview mirror and saw my daughter's face slump in sadness. I read so much in that moment.

"Mommy, I communicate in a way that's comfortable for me."

"Mommy, I show you my love. Why do I have to tell you?"

"Mommy, I'm okay."

I decided to make a bold move that day. With my faith cradled in one hand and my determination in another, I choose to no longer subject her to exams and assessments outside of what was absolutely necessary for her IEP.

No more piercing eyes watching my daughter's every move, silently writing on a notepad – the same yellow notepad that all doctors must purchase together at some wholesale store.

Taking a stand was the most exhilarating thing I could have done for my daughter. We spent more time together and nurtured our relationship through bonding and the freedom that came from acceptance.

Two weeks later, I sat sitting at a table nestled in the nook of the Starbucks coffee house while my daughter flipped through the pages of her book. She turned a page, pointed out a few pictures, and said, "Star, blue, sky."

Almost in a daze, I turned towards her. Then she smiled and opened her little mouth and sang, "Twinkle, twinkle, little star, how I wonder what you are."

At that moment, that time stood still. I dropped to my knees and wrapped my arms around her little body. And there I was with tears streaming down my face, in the middle of Starbucks, singing Twinkle, Twinkle Little Star.

People approached me to hand me a tissue and see if Nevaeh was okay. But as they got closer they would turn away as if to respect the privacy of that unforgettable comment.

I decided I would use my own teaching styles techniques on my daughter and make it a loving experience. From that day forward, I have not gone back on my commitment to my daughter and have grown more proud of my twinkling little star.

Teaching Styles

Figure 3- Antoinette and Nevaeh studying.

Children learn in different ways. And although the maturity of the brain is an important factor when it comes to learning, the real story in retaining the information and applying it is slightly more complicated.

The way children learn depends on age, level of development and environment. Notice I said children and not special needs children. The three major types of learning described by behavioral psychology are classical conditioning, operant conditioning, and observational learning. (Cherry, 2019).

"If I learn a different way, if I socialize a different way, I cannot and will not let myself be stereotyped by anyone's small thinking. Everyone has the right to be comfortable and free to learn the way we need to without fear."

—Nevaeh, 11

When I walked into different care centers or learning centers, it seemed like every child and parent I met wanted the responsibility of autism given to someone else. I do not believe children should spend their childhood in a therapist's office. As parents, we should, instead, guide the process along by being involved with setting up goals and evaluating what treatments to consider.

When we are an integral part of the decision-making process, we can accurately measure what is working and what needs adjusting. Optimal child development requires the active engagement of adults who teach children about acceptable behavior, understanding and learning. (American Academy of Pediatrics, 2013).

"If a child can't learn the way we teach,
maybe we should teach the way they learn."

–Ignacio Estrada

Learning differences are also related to genetics, temperament and environment, but in this chapter, I will give you a high-level overview of my teaching techniques that helped my daughter shift from being nonverbal, having very little hand-eye coordination to no longer meeting the eligibility for autism.

After I saw an improvement with my daughter, from 2006-2013, I set out to find other studies that found similar results. I found two studies published in 2013 and 2014 that noted marked improvements of an individual with ASD

In 2013, University of Connecticut clinical psychologist Deborah Fein, published in the *Journal of Child Psychology and Psychiatry*. Dr. Fein's study noted "surprising and remarkable progress identifying 34 young people aged between 8 and 21 years who had achieved what she and her colleagues labeled an "optimal outcome." (Fein & Barton, 2013).

A year after, in 2014, clinical psychologist Catherine Lord, an autism expert at Weill Cornell Medical College in New York, followed up with a study that involved 85 children with autism they had followed from aged between 2 through 19 years. Although the study suggested more tests be administered, the findings concluded that 9 percent of the group no longer met diagnostic criteria for autism by age 19.

Success stories are taking place not only from my daughter, but also across the globe if given the right amount of belief and resilience. I believe if you build on my techniques, you will be rooted in the fundamental process of my intuition, research and best wishes for your children to thrive.

Remember, you have everything you need for your child. I will show you how by:

- Providing honest educational experiences that helped me with my daughter

- Illustrating how vital creativity, coupled with a sweet spirit of perseverance, will take you

Writing

One day I picked Nevaeh up early from elementary school, and I had the opportunity to speak with her and check in on Nevaeh's progress. I wanted to know what were the areas of improvement and how could I best support the class. The teacher said, "Nevaeh has more than autism; she has an intellectual disability that impacts her from making any shapes. I am afraid she is too weak to grasp a pencil."

I nodded and thanked her for her opinion and left school with my daughter before she could see my clinched fist. I was not about to let the declaration of a teacher be my reality.

As a mother, no one can see what I can see.

At some point I had gotten used to the perceptions of people and decided I was capable to overcome every challenge that presented itself. I owed it to my daughter and I owed it to myself. I decided to take off work that week.

I skipped to Ikea, bought a bistro set, came back home, and got to work. After two hours of messing around with screws and a tiny Allen wrench, and one broken nail, the set was complete. I gathered up all of Nevaeh's lovies and lined them against the wall of our tiny apartment. I picked up Nevaeh, kissed her, and sat her down at the table. Next, I dramatically laid a sheet of paper and pencil in front of her and twirled as I said, "Boys and girls we are in for a treat! Nevaeh is going to write a great feat!"

I pretended the teddy bears could clap and said, "Nevaeh, please grab the pencil for this demonstration." She did, but immediately dropped it as her fingers searched for their proper placement. We practiced her grasp for that day as the crowd of lovies of all shapes and sizes went wild.

The next day, I invited Nevaeh back for an encore and instructed her to draw a line on the paper. She drew a very faint line and smiled.

"One more, Nunu!"

With determination gleaming in her eyes she picked up the pencil, slowly wrapped her fingers around it and drew another shaky line. I looked at Nevaeh, and I said, "Baby, you can do this. You can do anything you set your mind to."

And for the first time, I saw Nevaeh begin to believe in herself.

The following day I said, "We are taking it up a notch, Nevaeh. This will be our final act!" I smiled and excitedly said, "You are going to write the letter 'N' for Nevaeh." I demonstrated how to do it. Then I let her try. She dropped the pencil. This time I put my hand over her hand and guided her by making the lines together.

We tried one time, two times, then three and Nevaeh got overwhelmed and flapped her hands frantically. With tears in her eyes, she picked up the pencil and tossed it across the room.

I stepped away, stunned. *Did I push her too hard too soon?*

With a deep breath, I picked up the pencil, handed it to her and said, "Let's go. Draw the letter 'N'".

Nevaeh slammed her little hand on the desk and tossed the pencil across the room again – but this time I made her pick it up. She stomped over to the pencil and came back to the table.

I remember thinking, *ahh, there she is. There's my little temper tantrum throwing child. Good, give me all that energy and let's get to work.* In that moment I removed the autism expectation or enablement from my daughter and set it apart from the child I was determined to teach and led.

When she sat back down at the table, I gathered my breath, placed both hands on the table and asked, "Are you a winner or a loser?" Nevaeh was nonverbal at the time, but again, the eloquence of her expression spoke volumes. I let her sit within that moment and watched as she thought about my question. Nevaeh's face traveled from emotion to emotion as she searched for the answer of who she was.

I asked again, "Nevaeh, are you a winner or a loser? If you're a winner pick up that pencil."

She picked up her pencil. I responded with, "Okay, let's win."

Nevaeh slowly curved her hand and moved the pencil. She stopped periodically to review her progress and compare with the example 'N' I had written on paper.

After a few minutes, Nevaeh placed the pencil down and sat with what she had written. She moved her hand slowly, almost in disbelief.

She had made the letter 'N'.

Nevaeh chose to be a winner.

From that point on, every time we went to a restaurant, I would ask her to write an 'N' on a napkin. When she joined me at a café, I asked her to write an 'N' on a coffee cup. Anywhere we went was fair game. The world was our canvas.

Eventually we worked our way up from an "N' to her entire name. Then her name evolved into other words and words into sentences. She proved herself to be a winner over and over again.

When your child has a breakthrough writing moment, it is imperative to follow up, to work on defining newly shaped behaviors for sustained success. Patience and practice are key to allowing your child to redefine who they are past what the doctor's report and diagnosis implies.

Add variety in your routine with your child as you follow-up in unexpected and spontaneous ways. The more unpredictable you are the more this helps you gain their trust and build confidence while helping them work on speed and agility.

More often than not, the issue is not with our children, it is with us as parents. We let the neurodevelopment disorder be the reason why we do not encourage and awaken excellence in our children.

When patience leaves us, the vision of our children becomes stifled. We have to remind ourselves that our children do not have the life experiences yet to know what tenacity, perseverance, or grit is. They are counting on us to pull it out of them and prepare them to make better choices.

Chaos World

Most people with autism have a very limited amount of attention span with a unique sensitivity to sound. To a child with ASD, the sounds of the world create chaos.

I wanted Nevaeh to feel like she could handle anything thrown her way, even the small sound of a ticking clock or the loud laughter of a family member that often bothered her.

I introduced this chaotic world to her, five minutes at a time. While Nevaeh did her homework, I would play music and slowly increase the volume. As soon as the music distracted Nevaeh from her task, I lowered the volume. We did this every time during homework, or while she was reading or coloring and sometimes during our Heaven Fun Dome. As long as Nevaeh's focus was on a task, I knew I could slowly, thoughtfully, and respectfully introduce new sounds and music at various volume levels to help build her tolerance.

As time went on, Nevaeh was no longer bothered by noises she used to run from. The same child who used to run and scream from the noise of a vacuum was now helping me vacuum while shouting "turn the music up."

I felt like a perfect mixture between She-Hulk, a mad scientist, and a devoted mother.

But more than anything else, I was so thrilled that Nevaeh had the ability to be less affected from noises that would otherwise hurt her.

I invite you to start small. Try playing music softly while your child sleeps at first. The following day, while she is reading, play the same set of sounds you played from the night before and gradually increase the volume. Test the length of time and volume level until you and your child have found a comfortable balance.

Remember to do this methodically and respectfully. Because many children with ASD are sound sensitive, you need to treat this with the ultimate care. If you do not have a handle on Chaos World, or you feel uncertain, don't force it on your child. You can continue to play different sounds like white noise or jazz while she sleeps, but practice on a friend or family member until you have struck the right chord.

Manipulatives

Before you bought a purse or bag, did you need to feel the texture of the leather? Before you bought a suit or a shirt, did you need to run the material through your hands to feel if it meet your quality standards before you went ahead and dropped some serious cash on it?

If yes, manipulatives are very similar in allowing a hands on experience in the decision making process.

Manipulatives are colorful objects given to children as a hands-on way of problem solving. Children with autism are substantially better than average with visual stimuli and respond better with retaining information when vibrant visuals and textures are used. (Foss-Feig, Tadin, Schauder, & Cascio, 2013).

Allowing children to manipulate learning tools is an ideal way of teaching children in general, however allowing children with ASD to feel and manipulate the texture of what they are learning is an ideal educational environment given how their wonderful minds operate. (Merin, Young, Ozonoff, & Rogers, 2007). As you have learned in Chapter 1, *The Structure of the Human Brain*, and Chapter 2, *What is Autism Spectrum Disoder*, the mind of a person with ASD is physiologoically different at no fault of their own. And, in fact, they are better suited to out-of-the-box teaching and teaching methods.

Color Psychology

"And all the colors I am inside have not been invented yet."

-Shel Silverman

Color psychology is a well-known yet less explored branch of how our brain understands what it visualizes. In other words, do we understand the things we see and how do colors affect our understanding?

Next time you are in a room, look around and see how the colors of the place make you feel. How does being in a red room make you feel over a room filled with blue colors?

For example:

- The color blue gives us a feeling of serenity and peace.
- Red signifies passion.
- Brown provides us with a sense of dependability.
- Yellow is for energy.

On your next job interview or important business meeting, you might want to consider a color combination of brown and blue. By doing so, you will provide a sense of peaceful dependability. The impact that colors have on our minds shapes our decision making by cutting deep into our emotions and splashing all over our cognition.

Taking the understanding of color psychology with the tool of manipulatives, I developed what is similar to an educationally charged high-intensity interval training (HIIT) workout. HIIT is a cardiovascular exercise strategy alternating short periods of intense anaerobic exercise with less severe recovery periods, until too exhausted to continue (Laursen and Jenkins, 2013).

Now, my HIIT workout called **Heaven Fun Dome** did not exhaust Nevaeh, but it kept her in a consistent state of moving and thinking will developing her skills.

Heaven Fun Dome

I went on Amazon and bought every colored block, tube, foam, and dye that seemed to meet my requirements. If I was going to use this with my daughter, my most precious gift in this world, I needed everything to be perfect.

Once my supplies came in, I felt like it was Christmas morning. I laughed at every neighbor's raised brow as I rushed inside on the tips of my toes with my packages. I am sure they thought I was running some secret business out of my home, but I could not contain my excitement, I knew Nevaeh, and I were going to change the game.

I moved my couch against the wall and built our Heaven Fun Dome, as shown in Figure 10.

Figure 4 Illustration of Heaven Fun Dome

Heaven Fun Dome was a sensory safe half-moon circuit constructed in the middle of my living room floor where Nevaeh sat in the middle with five separate workout spaces within reach. Each workout was color coordinated and lasted for two minutes for optimal performance.

Workout 1 – Colors

I taught Nevaeh primary colors like yellow, red, and blue using food dye and water. Nevaeh and I took turns adding food dye to the water, and we watched as the water transformed.

To teach Nevaeh secondary colors, I would freeze ice cubes of colors to add them into warm water so she could see what color combination produced.

- Yellow ice cubes went into red water to make orange.
- Red ice cubes went into blue water to make purple.
- Blue ice cubes went into yellow water to make green.

This workout gave Nevaeh a chance to watch, develop, and take shape in a way that was tangible for her.

Workout 2 – Problem Solving

When the timer went off, we moved to problem-solving. I placed arithmetic flashcards on the floor like 2 + 2 = 4 and other basic math equations. Just below each flashcard, would be different manipulatives like-colored pasta, color-coded cotton balls, and Legos. In the case of 2+2=4, I had Nevaeh take two pieces of pasta along with two pieces of cotton balls as a way for her to essentially feel the weight of addition.

The same concept applied to subtraction and eventually multiplication. I found that as long as Nevaeh could manipulate the math equations, she welcomed the learning process and wanted to keep going.

Workout 3 – Dance Party

I set the timer during this period to play the type of music that would bring Nevaeh to her feet after completing Chaos Word. It's no secret that dancing can do a lot for mood improvement and mobility. Not only that, when I was growing up, I wanted to be a professional ballet dancer, so I joined in on the fun with Nevaeh as we danced together.

Our dance party was a way to reduce Nevaeh's anxiety and prepare her for her next task.

Workout 4 – Speed Reading/Writing

This workout allowed for one minute of Nevaeh finding the misspelled sight words I placed on the floor and then the other minute to rewrite the wrong words after finding them.

Workout 5 – Cool Down

30 Second Deep Breathing

Most of us breathe incorrectly, especially when we are stressed. To correct this, I asked Nevaeh to think about her belly like a balloon and to breathe in deep to fill the balloon, and breathe out to deflate it.

1 Minute of: Shaving Cream Play, Slime Play in Ziploc or Shaking a Glitter Jar

Immediately after her breathing practice, I let Nevaeh choose which sensory play she wanted. Believe it or not, shaving cream is very soothing when you rub or play with it. And for many kids, slime is equally weird as it is relaxing for the same reason watching glitter swirl is impressive. Most kids need to feel or see a new type of texture or display of patterns to engage several parts of the brain as they are learning.

Ending with 30 Seconds of mama bear hugs with loud affirmations.

The workouts always ended with my loving on Nevaeh and reminding her just how awesome and amazing she was.

The measurement of each workout lasting only two minutes provided a steady stream of focus for ten consecutive minutes all the while improving Nevaeh's attention span. Not only that, Nevaeh had to do her best to describe what she was doing and why. Being vocal helped her fine-tune her language and social skills. Nevaeh was also able to activate her motor skills by moving the objects around while engaging in scientific reasoning.

Please know that an activity that is perfectly stimulating for one child may be under- or over-stimulating for another. You will need to gauge the response and feel where your child is on the sensory threshold.

Out of the five exercises, Nevaeh's favorite workout typically the dance party and cooling down with shaving cream. The dance break was essential to me as I got to see how Nevaeh's movement increased in fluidity while she was able to cool herself down with the texture of shaving cream being her reward.

Once you tailor your workouts at home below are the critical areas for you to look and engage in creative opportunity. Out of the many advantages of engaging sensory play, these are the top five areas you will see a marked improvement on faster:

- Language skills – children improve their language skills as they talk about their experiences.
- Social skills – children who engage in sensory experiences learn to express themselves using descriptive adjectives.
- Fine motor skills – as children manipulate small objects they are building on the muscles and flexibility within their grasp
- Scientific reasoning skills – children learn about cause and effect when handling sensory materials.
- Self-control skills – children develop self-control as they learn to respect the rules and boundaries for sensory play while having fun.

Everyday Mechanics

Our daily activities consist of so much movement that we often forget how we train our bodies. Movements like driving a car, answering the phone or even tossing popcorn into our mouths allow fun ways to practice and improve our body's mechanics.

We have covered the challenges people with ASD face in communication, so now is the time for a gentle reminder along with my teaching methods.

Reinforcing the importance of communication along with **everyday mechanics** of our behaviors will help you gain an intuitive grasp on how you can best support your child going forward.

Everyday activities also help develop fine motor skills and hand-eye coordination. I encouraged my daughter to try out everyday tasks to help her improve her skills.

Tasks you may consider around the home include:
- Baking
- Mopping
- Gardening

Tasks you may consider with personal care include:

- Brushing teeth
- Getting dressed
- Tying shoelaces

Please also consider this, while it may be faster for you to complete your household and cooking tasks yourself, you do a disservice by not including your children. We should try to not be in so much of a rush to get things done that we miss the opportunity for wonderful teaching and bonding moments with our little ones.

Set aside extra time at a minimum once a week, where you can make corrections in your children in a fun way.

Baking:

Baking is my favorite activity to do with my daughter. When we bake together, we get the opportunity to combine science, math, patience, and fine motor skills – and you get a sweet reward at the end. Every time we baked our cupcakes me heart swelled with pride when Nevaeh would pipe the tops of them with the icing we had made ourselves. It meant her grasp had improved.

Mopping:

Have you ever mopped your floor and see how tired it makes you? The sweeping motion of mopping requires hand-eye coordination with fine motor skills in action.

Sometimes when Nevaeh would mop the floor, I would set the timer and make it a game to see if she could beat her score. Every moment is an opportunity to experience more and improve.

Gardening:

Gardening is a delicate scientific approach to the idea of cause and effect. The texture of the cool soil was something Nevaeh greatly enjoyed. Not only that, she could see quite literally the fruit of her labor when we planted in winter and picked our fruit in the spring.

Brushing teeth:

Brushing our teeth requires a great deal of synchronization between visual and motor skills then we think.

Getting dressed:

Putting on clothes and fastening buttons and zippers helps improve hand-eye coordination, motor skills, and a sense of confidence in self-independence.

Tying shoelaces:

In-hand manipulation is slightly different than other fine motor skill activities and may be more difficult.

If your child is having a particularly rough time with zippers or fastening their buttons, try clothes that slip on and have Velcro or snap-on buttons. Choose what you think might be a better priority to focus on with your children. For me, I didn't care if she could tie her shoelaces if her social skills were improving. I could easily buy a pair of trendy slip-on shoes and keep it pushing.

Check-in point

I shared all of the above to illustrate that as a parent, you will need to feel the moment to push the envelope and intuitively glean when it is time to pull back.

Can you think of moments you have seen your child interact with you? Please take the time to write them below:

_____

_____

_____

_____

_____

_____

_____

How can you support your child?

_____

_____

_____

What are some everyday activities you can incorporate
with your children?

_____

_____

_____

_____

_____

_____

_____

_____

Fail Big and Fail Often

"... far too often, epidemically often, we go for the external win at the cost of our internal wellness. And that's because we don't value our inner attunement as much as we value outer attainment."

— Author Unknown

An important life lesson for anyone to learn is how to think like a winner. A winner is meticulously shaped, groomed, and taught to tackle the ordinary to achieve the extraordinary. We have to make room for our children to fail big and fail often to have the confidence and mental strength to keep trying.

An enormous challenge within the special needs community is not allowing our children's diagnosis to be the measuring rod of success. When we allow ourselves to buy into expectation, we morph into enablers who accept bad behaviors under the guise of autism.

Autism does not steer the ship; your child is her own captain and she will steer that ship through any storm as long as she has the foundational fortitude and confidence to do so drilled in at an early age.

I have heard so many parents coddle their children and accept failure by blaming the diagnosis instead of pushing their children towards excellence. I never said to my daughter, "Oh, you have autism, honey, and it is okay if you don't get it right. I am just glad you tried." No excuses.

The day my daughter chose to hold her pencil and write is the day she decided to be a winner. In my house, we win. And in order to feel a true win, we have to know what failure looks, feels, and tastes like.

Failing allows us to establish a balance in our lives. Failing does not equate a failure of a person, but a failure moment to build the unique taste for the desire to win.

After years of working on Nevaeh's hand-eye coordination and spatial awareness, I figured it was time to place her in competitive sports. We started with basketball at the urging of my friends who recognized how tall my daughter was and felt her height would give her an advantage in the game.

We went to practice, rain or shine and Nevaeh got better. She loved it and loved the opportunity to make more friends. Not only that, the team was on a winning streak. But just like most streaks they eventually come to an end.

Nevaeh's team did not win their championship game.

I remember that game like it was yesterday. The game was tied, and both teams were playing strong. I ran up and down the bleachers cheering for the team. I almost lost my mind yelling, "Post up, post up," or "D up!" They were playing to win.

The clock on the buzzer was steady running out, with 5 seconds to go, I grabbed another parent as the visiting team caught the ball. With 3 seconds on the clock, the young lady made a shot, and it went right in the basket as the time ran out — game point.

That ride home was difficult. It was the first time Nevaeh had lost a game, and she was going hard on herself. The coach called us on the way home and invited us to a ceremony that following Saturday for the girls to receive their trophies.

I remember asking, "Why is the team getting a trophy if they did not win?"

The coach said, "We just want to encourage the girls because they played a good game."

"I agree. I'm so proud of Nevaeh. But I'm sorry, we won't be attending."

All of a sudden chaos erupted in my car. The coach yelled on the phone and said I was unreasonable, my daughter yelled, "This isn't fair" and the backseat driver, my mother, said, "Stop being hard on my grandbaby."

I'm glad I didn't snap. Honestly, I could care less about the feelings of anyone else. I knew my daughter had an amazing road to climb and we were not taking any handouts to get there.

I wanted Nevaeh to value every trophy, every win she made. Winners are made through hard work, perseverance, healthy minds, and the will to succeed, not based on handouts because you failed.

Since that day of Nevaeh not getting a trophy, she turned into a competitive dream showing true sportsmanship.

The same girl that had very little hand-eye coordination was dominating in volleyball, basketball and softball. Nevaeh has a whole wall dedicated to trophies she paid in blood and sweat equity.

Doubting yourself as a parent is normal. Wondering when to push and when to pull back is a delicate tango that eventually you will learn the rhythm and cadence of.

Verbal and Nonverbal: Can't We All Just Get Along?

Relate is the root word of relationship. To relate, we must be excellent communicators; however, sadly, poor communication between parents is widespread. Allow me to introduce you to the other side of the fight — the verbal vs. non-verbal conflict between parents. Yes, it's a thing.

When Nevaeh was in elementary school, I was on the classroom committee with two other parents, discussing decorations for the holidays. As with most calls like this, usually one parent will ask another about their child's progress, and it will turn into an all-out therapy session.

When I was expressing my challenges, a mother interrupted me furiously.

"Oh, what are you complaining about? You have NOTHING to complain about. At least your daughter is verbal! My son Joe doesn't say a single thing to me, ever! Who do you think you are?!"

I sat on the phone, shocked for a minute.

I said, "I think I am the mother of a child who WAS nonverbal for years, and now I am trying to get her to her next goal."

Verbal versus nonverbal is an actual issue breed from us lacking sympathy or compassion and expecting preferential treatment if we are suffering more.

As parents and caregivers to our children, the majority of the work we do is not found in hard data but gathered intuitively. And while we allow ourselves to be guided gently by an inexplicable calling, we also leave exposed points of vulnerability.

Whether we are looking for critiques, comments, or judgments, we have it thrown our way. And the worry or concern we have never fades – it shifts to another high level of security.

When my daughter was nonverbal, I worried something would happen to her, and she would not be able to tell me.

And now, on the other side of the verbal fence, I get:

"Your child doesn't even look autistic."
"Oh, she's normal now!"
"Wait, is Nevaeh cured?!"

Either way, do not allow yourself to feel like you have to campaign at all times and correct anyone you come into contact with that isn't aware of what autism is. Don't feel the need to engage or correct. There is grace in letting go and maintaining your own happiness.

Misery loves company, but you have better things to do like take over the world by advocating for the needs of your child.

Autism and Schools

I am going to do my best and not make this chapter about bashing our school system or pointing out the disparities with underserved schools and neighborhoods. While these are very real issues, I will, instead create space to focus lawful needs of our children and creating harmony within the school and family life.

There comes the point in every mother's life when she says, "I'm TIRED!" Tired of the school system's crazy days off, incessant donation drives and the miscommunication of the school districts. It's not any fault for one specific person or entity but rather a result of overcrowded schools and not enough support.

Below is what every mother with a child with a special-eligibility has asked:

Should I put my kid in a public school on the alternate curriculum?

Should I put my kid in a high functioning autism program?

Should I put my kid in core autism curriculum?

Is the bell system to loud?

What is the ratio of special-education student to mainstreamed student?

How many classes can I safely mainstream from SPED classes?

Can I find a middle school with an assigned stable psychologist and not on rotation?

How do I make sure intervention support is on standby?

Do I immerse my child into general education and forego my IEP?

Should my child have full inclusion?

Should they be mainstreamed?

There is a ton of information to consider. And it can be very overwhelming. The only way to stay above water with this is to become aware of the special education process and your state's county laws. The more information you have, the better decisions you can make in the educational career of your child.

More than three decades have passed since Hendrick Hudson Central School District v. Rowley. The Supreme Court's interpretation of FAPE – Free Appropriate Public Education – concluded that students with special needs are not entitled to the best possible education but one that met their basic needs. (Bitsika & Sharpley, 2016).

According to Patricia Horan Latham, J.D., author of Special Education Law, the "free" in FAPE means that all eligible students with disabilities will be educated at public expense. There is no cost to the parent. Appropriate means that your child is entitled to an education to meet her needs as stated within the Individualized Education Program (IEP). Public refers to whatever the nature of your child's eligibility or determination; he or she is has the right to be educated under public supervision and not cast aside. FAPE ensures that your kiddo will receive the support services they qualify for and will prepare your child for higher education, employment, and independent living.

Once your child has met the eligibility for autism, there are laws of protection for the rights of your baby. Please get to know FAPE and IDEA fully so you can see just how supported you are. In my case, the particular school we attended at the time was not upholding the student rights a week.

The teacher said, "Ms. Banks, you don't have to drop by the classroom so often. I know you're uncomfortable with my classroom for your daughter. But we have it handled."

I said, "What exactly does 'have it handled' mean? There has been no improvement in my daughter. She never receives any homework. So, unfortunately, yes, I do have to drop by. I have to slip away on my lunch break to drop off an assignment for my daughter to work on because you are not doing enough." The truth is, I would often submit packets for Nevaeh to study while in the classroom. I am sure the teacher did not appreciate it. It wasn't my goal to aggravate the situation, but I was done with trying her methods. I could not risk stagnation in my daughter's learning.

Many schools adhere to teaching outdated methods, filled to the brim with standardized tests and cookie-cutter assessments. Students get rewarded for memorization, not imagination or resourcefulness, so it's up to you to set the standard.

I was not satisfied with the level of lawful commitment my child was due. I hired over five different attorneys that ended up charging a ridiculous amount of money without securing the results I needed. I was broke, in debt and frustrated. Just as I was almost to my breaking point, I picked up the phone one last time and ended up striking gold. This attorney ended up helping me file for process hearing and mediation with my daughter's school district.

An excerpt from my letter:

"Because my complaint involves a matter which calls for direct State Department of Education intervention pursuant to Title 5 of the California Code of Regulations Section 4650(a)(7), I have not filed with the local district. Instead, I request direct state intervention in this matter.

I ask for immediate investigation and resolution, as my daughter cannot afford to wait for these services.

You have every right to request progress updates on established goals. And if anything does not make sense, then ask for more information. You have the right to push back on objectives you feel do not where you know in your heart your child can go. Autism is not a label you accept and let the chips fall where they may. Autism is a neurodevelopmental disorder that requires a specific way of communication and learning environment. I am raising my daughter to be a leader and words like disabled, disadvantaged, or displaced are not even an option.

I would also like to caution you against allowing your child's IEP to be the only measuring rod you focus on. There are so many points to an IEP and the overall development of your child that it's easy to allow the letter grade to fall by the wayside.

You have to pay just as close attention towards the social, development goals along with requiring academic excellence for your kiddos.

One of the hardest things for children with IEP's and in special education is maintaining a really great balance between all they're up against. Please also don't allow excuses to fall into place. You simply cannot convince yourself that academic goals are less important than IEP's goals. Conversely IEP goals are not less important than academic.

Any modification you may need might indicate a change in the course, standard, test preparation, location, timing, scheduling, expectation, student response, or other attributes that provide your child with the best environment to get what they need.

Take your time and review all options. Don't be overwhelmed, definitely ask as many questions you need.

Imminent Loneliness

While advocating for our children, we adapt to our "new normal" and live our life the best that we can. We tend to have more numbers for therapists, physicians, physician's assistants, coaches and care providers than we do for real friends. Admitting that is hard. Because as rockstars in the development of our children, the road becomes lonely after the lights, camera, action is done.

I had my daughter when I was twenty. Right at the beginning of a decade of what should have been about finding myself, college dorm life and making wrong decisions, I found myself through motherhood. I grew as my child did.

The majority of my friends did not have children and they often wanted to hang out late in the evening. And, while I appreciated the invitation and loved to entertain the possibility of being able to go out, I had to decline.

Sometimes friends would invite me and tell me to bring my daughter, but how could I when the majority of the time, I would be worried about her comfort?

I did not feel up for the challenge to make excuses for my daughter if she would need a moment, if she did not feel like communicating, or if the sounds around us were too hard for her to bear.

If you are raising a child with autism, everything I have described you already know and feel on an emotional level. You know that going out to eat is almost impossible. You know all about the sleepless nights, the meltdowns and the judgments that come your way.

At times you feel so separated from the world that you're not sure you fit in it anymore because you have had to adapt in such a complicated way. The conversations from other parents at school or in your social group are filled with regular school outings, shopping, and what's new with the hottest celebrity, while all you really want to talk about is the latest in special education laws, how your child can withstand loud noises now or you're absolutely terrified of the next classroom field trip.

You have no clue what those around you are talking about because your days are filled with therapy, special education, and all the other latest methods that are proving to be a hit in the autism world.

And when you have managed to pull yourself out of the loneliness tunnel, before you know it, you are back in.

So, what do you do? You hide that loneliness.

We learn how to hide it. We struggle through it and move on as the world moves on. We conceal our loneliness behind our smiles and embrace each day for what it is. Not everyone gets the chance to raise an angel in disguise.

Time for a shift.

To gain a sense of myself back, I first started unpacking who I was as a woman. If I was going to read the latest research applications for autism, then I was also going to read about the latest make-up techniques, fashion, and woman entrepreneur tips. I decided to make my world revolve around a balanced level of excellence.

This time I decided to not only be the best mother I could be, but the best woman.

Interestingly enough, as my daughter started progressing, so did my outward appearance. I let go of my go-to ponytail and started wrapping my hair at night to cut down on my morning routine, and as we both practiced in excelling in autism and motherhood, Nevaeh and I started gleaming like it was no one's business.

And then I was and still am slammed with, "Antoinette, why aren't you married?"

I think about that time and time again. It's certainly not for lack of trying, I would have preferred a partner with in the daily battles and triumphs. I have met quality men, but for me, it just took a little more. I suppose I have not felt like I had an equal partner to actively support what it meant for me to be an advocate for my daughter.

Could he attend an IEP meeting? Sure. But more than ever, I would have loved for a partner to take an active interest in the latest research methods or have ideas to bounce off of. I felt I did not have the time to maintain a fighting stance for my child while simultaneously bringing someone up to speed with what autism was. At the time, I did not have it in me.

Loneliness in most single mothers is overshadowed by what must get done daily. The stress of bills, managing schedules, work, and school activities are often a mixture of tiredness that are inseparable because relationships don't cure stress or loneliness — just aloneness.

I did not want to spend the time away from my daughter, arrange a baby sitter, and put away my note cards and progress reports on someone just for a date. In my eyes, it just was not worth the risk.

My daughter has said, "Mommy, can you get married so someone and be here and love you and have your back the way you got mine?"

I thought that was so sweet that she considered me. I said to her, "Sweetheart, Mommy will get married when I am comfortable with his consistency and dependability and I am waiting for the right man who will love you the way I do."

Loneliness hurts. Rejection hurts. Losing someone hurts. Love is the medium that covers and grants patience through the pain. And the love you have for your children will continue to carry you through this autism journey.

Loneliness in Your Children

> *"Mommy. It's hard to make friends when their minds and souls aren't sound."*
>
> -   *Nevaeh, age 9*

Most people experience is this incredible desire to belong. We all want to feel accepted, loved and cherished for who we are. Our children with ASD are indeed the same. We have to consider is that although our children present to enjoy their alone time and the world they live in, they do get lonely sometimes.

Although you may think your son or daughter prefers their space and the beautiful world they live in, regardless if they tell you or not, our children experience loneliness on a deeper level.

Building a connection with someone requires communication skills, empathy, picking up on social cues and shared interests. Imagine how more challenging that might be to a person who experiences socialization in a profoundly different way (Morales et al., 2000).

To the world, our ASD children may seem as if they are disconnected. Both children and adults with autism also tend to have difficulty interpreting what others are thinking and feeling and sometimes develop a social phobia and general anxiety (Salazar et al., 2015). Subtle social cues such as a smile, wave, or grimace may convey little meaning. Without the ability to interpret gestures and facial expressions, the social world can seem bewildering.

What can you do?

> *"The phoenix must burn to emerge."*
>
> *– Janet Fitch*

While I respected my daughter's interests, I did not allow her to opt-out of experiences because of the anxiety from being social. "The tougher, the better" was my motto. I remember distinctively telling my daughter if we could push ourselves right outside our comfort zones that is when the magic happens, authentic experience of life and learning. I asked her to trust me and follow my lead. But as with most young one's growing up, the older they got, the more they pushed back.

One day we were on the way to her All-Girls Robotics club, and Nevaeh says, "Mommy, I don't want to go. There will be so many people there. The noises will hurt my ears. Please, mom! Can't I watch anime at home where it's quiet?"

"No," I said softly while still driving towards the valley.

"Mom, please! I don't want to do this, why are you making me do this? I'm not any good at it and no one likes me anyway."

I looked at my daughter's face that looked so uncomfortable and sad. I was reminded of the same face when she had enough with the testing and therapy sessions. But this was different. I could not allow Nevaeh to cower and cave in. And, I hated seeing her in any sort of pain or discomfort. I wanted to give in and grant her everything she asked. I wanted to call the instructor and tell her we would not make, make a beeline to the grocery store, grab some snacks, put on Netflix and veg out. I wanted her safe, I wanted her happy, and most importantly, I did not want to be her villain.

I took a deep breathe, and steeled my mom-heart as best as I could and said again, "No."

She whined and said, "That is so unfair! I can't do any of the things they want me to do. I am not any good! Why do you keep making me do things when you know I am not good?"

And with the feeling of a thousand mothers roar inside me, I said, "You will give this a shot. You will give me four solid meetings. Afterward, if you still don't like it, I won't take you. But, check this out – the next time I hear you say one bad thing about yourself again, I will make you run alongside this car. Am I understood?!"

"Yes, Mom."

Repeat after me:

I am smart
> *I am smart*

I am strong
> *I am strong*

I am capable
> *I am capable*

I do not make excuses
> *I do not make excuses*

I keep my commitments
> *I keep my commitments*

We made our way to the robotics club. As the day went on, I saw Nevaeh learning the hang of it. And with the concerted effort of the girls, they started to make the robot they had assembled move. With excitement, the girls cheered, hugged Nevaeh and high-fived each other.

I was so thrilled in seeing Nevaeh feel like one of the team. I put my sunglasses on to hide my tears from across the room. I wanted to run across the room and tell her how amazing she was, but instead, I gave Nevaeh a discreet thumbs up.

I enrolled Nevaeh into anything and everything I could get my hands on. Karate? We were there. Sports? We were there. Birthday parties, Girl Scouts, All-Girls Robotics team? We were there! I could see my daughter start to gain her confidence and create meaningful relationships. Nevaeh found her voice, and she found her own amazing personality and people loved her for it.

Truthfully, it meant my social life was nonexistent, and I felt like a chauffeur and personal assistant on most days but who cares if it meant my daughter could have every possible opportunity available to her?

Pushing past feelings and bringing logic to emotions can best allow the relationship with your children to grow as it did with me and my daughter.

I encourage you to bring as many new experiences to your child and push the envelope a little further. The overexposure to a variety of different ideas was the best thing I could have ever done. A mind that is stretched by a new experience can never go back to its old dimensions.

Support Group Realness

"Emotional pain is not something that should be hidden away and never spoken about. There is truth in your pain, there is growth in your pain, but only if it's first brought out into the open."

—Steven Aitchison

Needing support as I walked down the yellow brick road, balancing motherhood and the world of autism, was such a profound discovery process.

I wanted my family to get it. I wanted my friends to get it.

I wanted to not have to beg someone to attend an IEP meeting with me or a conference about Nevaeh's school or programs. I wanted them to show up and be there. Just, get it.

If I had to fight my daughter's teachers or her therapist, if I had to advocate daily, pop up to school, meet with principals—why on earth did I have to put on my boxing gloves at home?

Recently my grandmother told me she was afraid of my daughter when she was little. My grandmother said, "You know Antoinette, I was scared of Nevaeh when she would not speak. I did not know what to do with her. She frightened me."

My grandmother was a woman I admired so much and to hear her say this about someone I birthed, nurtured and gave my very best to snatched all the air out of my body. I started recounting moments over the years where my grandmother would make small judgmental remarks, nitpick, or be dramatic. It all made sense.

My response to my grandmother was, "After all this time, why did you choose to tell me now? Is it because you see how amazing Nevaeh is? You should have kept that one to yourself. I can't help you with your regret or guilt." I walked away.

Now that I'm in my thirties, I am filled with confidence and unapologetic. I refuse to internalize opinions that are not asked for or offered in love. At the end of the day, as much as a person might try, nobody knows how serious your life is to you, but you.

In Judith Johnson's and William McCown's book, Family Therapy of Neurobehavioral Disorders, they state: "Although support and self-help groups can vary greatly, all groups share one thing in common—they are places where people can share personal stories, express emotions, and be heard in an atmosphere of acceptance, understanding, and encouragement. Participants share information and resources. By helping others, people in a support group strengthen and empower themselves."

In my support group I found a safe place to ask questions, such as:

When was the time to be stern and hard?

When could I be gentle and kind?

When can I stop being Superwoman and simply be a wonderful woman?

Did I take on a more dominate personality to be both mother and father for my daughter?

Did the abuse I encountered as a child make me overprotective of who I allowed in my daughter's life? Was I healed?

Could I let my guard down?

Did I let my past define me?

Did I truly believe I was an overcomer?

Am I enough?

I constantly asked so many soul-searching questions because I never wanted to be shocked by my own response to unexpected moments. I went through my teens with a chip on my shoulder. I was mad at the world for my childhood experiences and even madder at myself for not being married and raising a child on my own.

I found my support group gave the space to ask questions that others would have considered "too much." I was given the space to explore my feelings without judgment from friends or my church community. I always walked away feeling empowered. I was proud I could ask myself tough questions and thrilled at the thought of myself blossoming more into a fearless woman.

Outside of the physical support group I attended, I found mothers all over the world that I connected with on social media. As soon as my daughter and I launched our support pages on Facebook and Instagram, I met wonderful mothers who shared in my experiences. Every women that fell under the hashtag umbrella of #autismmom #singlemother #singlemotherofcolor grew to be my extended family and best friends.

If you feel isolated in your community, search for a particular niche community that understands your needs. You're going to have to cut yourself and your family some slack if they don't particularly "get it."

Your friends and family mean well. They do. But remember that your friends and family are not experts in the reality of your life and believe it not, someone else wants the job you are trying to force on someone. People innately want to be a support as long as you allow the space for someone to give.

A Warrior Mom

"To live is to choose. But to choose well, you must know who you are and what you stand for, where you want to go and why you want to get there."

-Kofi Annan

On November 17, 2006, at 4:51 AM, my world was forever changed. I was a 20-year-old new mom, looking down at my daughter, who was swaddled in hospital blankets. I had never felt prouder. I brought this tiny treasure into the world, and I knew I would go to the ends of the earth for her.

Mama-bear instincts are real. And it's true, the moment we women give birth, we are changed past the feel-good emotions of oxytocin to make us bond faster with our children, and somehow, we women shed our cocoon and emerge as mothers with fierce emotions we never imagined.

Scientific American reports that pregnancy and lactation hormones may alter the brain, "increasing the size of the neurons in some regions and producing structural changes in others." (Scientific American, 2018).

I had accepted my calling to be a mother. It did not matter that I was single and that I, by all accounts, was ridiculed for not marrying my daughter's father. I knew I was not meant to hide behind the shadows of a fledgling marriage and that my daughter deserved a happy mother.

Interestingly enough, I like to believe that I was set up for the fight of my life with my daughter. I had experienced hardship as a young girl, steeled myself against ridicule for being pregnant at young age, and somewhere along the lines I transformed into a warrior — a fighter with a resilient mind poised for the brawl of a lifetime.

"I am aware that many object to the severity of my language; but is there no cause for severity? I will be as harsh as truth and as uncompromising as justice. On this subject, I do wish to think, or to speak, or write with moderation. No! No! Tell a man whose house is on fire to give a moderate alarm; tell him to moderately rescue his wife from the hands of the ravisher; tell the mother to gradually extricate her babe from the fire into which it has fallen....but urge

me not to use moderation in a cause like the present. I am in earnest---I will not equivocate---I will not excuse---I will not retreat a single inch---- AND I WILL BE HEARD"!!

–William Loyd Garrison

One of the significant gifts you receive when you embark on the journey of autism is that we discover ourselves all together. Many mothers view their children as a tragedy in their life. Parents target their kids for all the intangible fear and frustration there are facing in their lives.

Like arrows in the hands of a warrior are children born in one's youth.

-Psalm 127:4

To be a mother is to be a warrior — an archer. We leap up against our opposition, back rigid, and face taunt with our bow and arrow in hand.

I was hurt because I was a single parent.

I was in pain over the diagnosis of my child.

I was sad over the abandonment of my friends and family.

Every time I looked on social media, I saw perfectly glamorized photos of women who appeared to have it all together. And more importantly, while I was a mess sprinting from meeting to meeting and advocating for my daughter, I lost a little of the woman I was. So, in all that, I said, "Antoinette, get something for your pain. Get your return. Let your pain be for something!"

I badly wanted to combat the outcome of the doctor's report just like I needed air to breathe. I was not going to give up on daughter.

And so, like a warrior, I ignored the doctors and got to work.

Just as I knew I would go to the end of the earth for my daughter when she was born, I was reminded of that on her diagnosis day. I put on the full armor of God because for an archer, strength, endurance, and control were necessary.

With supernatural focus, I walked out onto the battlefield and in enemy territory. While the world raged, the warrior in me stood strong. I lifted my arms now strengthened from the fight to pull back my bow, prayed to God to guide the trajectory, and released the arrow of my daughter.

And every year the target changed. From the target of speech, the target of participation, of movement. The target of a life filled with quality.

Nevaeh, now a young lady, no longer meets the diagnostic criteria for autism. She hit every target set out before her accurately and with distinctive precision.

Nevaeh is on the honor roll, has won countless competitive trophies and wants to be a creator and director of films through the incredible perspective she has.

We were given our children because we are who they need. As mothers, we have the spirit of loving them on their hard days and the motivation and love to give them everything they need. You belong to them and they belong to you.

I thank God every day for selecting me to be the warrior mom of a miraculous activist and revolutionary. My prayer is that if you don't remember anything else; remember that labels come with a living, breathing, thriving person behind them.

Lessons My Daughter Taught Me

I remember waking up more very peacefully. I looked out my window and thought, *Ahh what a beautiful day it was. The birds were singing, the sun was shining so bright - wait. WHAT?! The sun ain't never that bright at 6:00AM.* I looked at my clock and felt my eyes jump out of my head as I leapt up out the bed.

I was late.

I rushed to put together breakfast, got Nevaeh dressed in her school uniform, and halfway got myself together. I drove past the other commuters and pulled into the school's driveway.

Great. I am 30 minutes behind schedule.

I jumped out of the car, grabbed my daughter, and dashed up the stairs to her preschool. Just as I was about to walk inside, Nevaeh starts crying.

"Oh, come on, Nugget. Not now, please. You'll be fine."

Nevaeh tries twisting out of my arms, in full tantrum mood. "Nevaeh, it's okay, honey. Please stop." Other parents are looking at us, a school administrator steps towards us, and I can feel myself getting red in the face.

Then, Nevaeh starts reaching for something.
I put her down and watch as she thoughtfully makes her way to a bed of flowers. Nevaeh's hand comes up slowly as she wipes her little face, looks at me, and then delicately touches a petal. I watch her smile at its texture. I knelt down to her level and placed her nose into the freshly bloomed flower. Nevaeh inhales deeply, looks at me as if inviting me to do the same. Together, Nevaeh and I smelled the roses.

How many times are we rushing through our days that we never, ever, stop to smell the roses?

In this particular segment of my book, we are going to talk about the lessons my daughter taught me so you can be sensitive to your developing relationship with your children.

- **Lesson 1:** Nothing should come between you and your child
- **Lesson 2:** They are a child, first
- **Lesson 3:** Trust them to be independent
- **Lesson 4:** Social anxiety is not just assigned to autism
- **Lesson 5**: Normalize the need to master social skills.
- **Lesson 6**: Give them an outside the box push.
- **Lesson 7**: Love unconditionally

Lesson 1: Nothing should come between you and your child.

I am incredibly privileged to have this amazing girl as my daughter. I love hard. I set the bar high. The way my relationship with my daughter is set up may not be for everyone to understand. Yet I hope it's a connection for every mother and child to feel.

My daughter and I have a, no-holds-barred approach with one another. We led with reality and do not sugar coat anything.

More than anything, I respect my daughter for exactly who she is. I have come to realize that because my daughter knows how much I love, admire and respect her, when I give her truth bombs, or when my language is not the best, she immediately snaps out of whatever rut, grants me grace as her mother, and finishes the task.

School administrator will call you and blame your child for not acting properly. Therapists will say your child is not succeeding as well as they should. Family members will say your child is rude because they have a difficult time with societal norms. But when you are tuned in to who your child is, you can intelligently speak to the problem and present a logical and holistic solution that is built on the respect and vision you have for your children.

Again, no one knows how serious your life is to you, but you.

Lesson 2: They are a child first.

"When I get to a new school or any kind of new environment, people knew of me but didn't really know me. After telling them what kind of classes I had people started identifying me as autistic. They didn't see me as a person; they saw me as a diagnosis."

- *Nevaeh, 12*

I never defined my daughter as autistic first. Instead, my daughter was a child first – a child who deserved unyielding love, compassion, happiness, and of course, fun.

Once the diagnosis of autism came, I had to differentiate between can't and won't. According to the doctors' reports and evaluations, my daughter could not do a myriad of things. However, together, we turned "can't" into "can

As Nevaeh got older, I learned to distinguish between "can't" and "won't." When my kiddo disagreed with me, did not want to eat all her veggies, or didn't pick up her toys, all of those moments were evidence of her growth as a child. Not an *autistic* child.

The diagnosis of autism should only come into play in the development modifications in socializing and academics that you will advocate for. In any other space, it is crucial to take a back seat and let your child drive who they are as a beautifully complex being.

Lesson 3: Trust them to be independent.

"Do not force your children to behave like you, for inevitably they have been created for a time which is different than your time."

- Author unknown

This notion of "letting go" can create so much anxiety, especially once we have become so used to anticipating every need of our child. It is far easier said than done when the time comes for us to allow room for our children's autonomy and independence.

Out of the many heart-pounding moments I've had, there are two I will share.

1st Occasion:

One Saturday morning I woke up to find Nevaeh and our poodle gone. Frantic, I called her cellphone, and she did not answer.

I quickly toss on a robe, I bust out of the apartment barefoot. I'm running, robe flying, with sleep in my eyes. Folks asked if I was ok while I zoomed past. I yelled back, "I'm looking for my daughter."

So many thoughts were going through my mind. Where is my daughter? *My baby, who gets lost easily. My baby, who is sensitive to high-pitched noises.*

I go to the three places where I think she could be: our building's library, the pool, or the park.

I went to the library, and no one had seen her. I jumped down a couple of stairs near the pool and scared the life out of a couple. I kept going moving until I got to the park where I found her letting our dog play with another dog. I dropped to my knees on the grass, most likely where a dog had peed.

Nevaeh sees me and comes rushing over. Out of breath, I said in a hoarse whisper, "Why are you here? You've got to ask my permission before you leave."

She says, "Mom, you said the dog was my responsibility. She needed to pee, and I didn't want to wake you. I was trying to be responsible."

Double gulp. Triple gulp. My blood pressure could not take that moment. I was impressed with her responsibility and sensitivity to me but completely overwhelmed. I was so happy to see Nevaeh safe and happy, even if that meant I looked like a crazy person.

2nd Occasion:

On our trip to the movies, Nevaeh decided she wanted snacks after we were already seated in the theater. As I was about to get up, Nevaeh jumps up and says, "I'll get them."

I looked at her pleading face and smiled, "Sure, baby. Be careful."

I sat on the edge of my seat until she came back. I watched her climb the steps with a massive amount of popcorn, huge Slurpee, and candy while I softly chanted "don't fall, don't fall, don't fall."

She sat down, proudly gave me my snacks and started eating hers, and I kissed her, held my forehead to hers, and thanked God for His promise.

I have used these moments to start a healthy dialogue. We have established rules: if Nevaeh wants independence, she will have to communicate when she has reached her destination, and when she's coming back. If not, I am sending the cavalry.

Lesson 4: Social anxiety is not only commissioned to autism

Can you think of a time your heart leapt into your stomach because you were about to go on a job interview, meet someone new, or do a presentation in front of an important group of people?

The majority of us could use guidance in social interactions. Research suggests anxiety disorders affect approximately 15 million American adults while the average age of onset happens during teenage years. (Kalat, 2016).

Most people who experience anxiety:
- Blush and feel a rapid heart rate
- Feel nauseous
- Show a rigid body posture,
- Make little eye contact
- Find it scary and confusing to be with other people
- Feel self-conscious in front of other people and feel flustered and uncomfortable

- Fear that other people will judge them
- Stay away from places where there are other people

As adults, to be a better parent for our children requires a sacrificing amount of vulnerability of who we are before we can pour into our children. We have to have honest conversations about our own challenges we face with fitting in and communicating with other people. Find friends we feel truly have our back while still maintaining our sanity.

Ask yourself what your biggest burdens were in trying to overcome your own anxiety and share them with your children, if you can. Sharing will show your child they are not alone in "normal" behavior and that everything is not unique to them because they have autism.

Lesson 5: Normalize the need to master social skills

Talking to kids about anxiety and mental health will help them understand they are not alone in social spaces. Most people lack in-depth social skills. Even the greatest public speakers have struggled with this anxiety. Scott Berkun explains these behaviors in his book, *Confessions of a Public Speaker.*

Our brains identify the following four things as being very bad for survival:

1. Standing alone
2. In open territory with no place to hide
3. Without a weapon
4. In front of a large crowd of creatures staring at you

"In the long history of all living things, any situation where all the above were true was very bad for you. It meant the odds were high that you would soon be attacked and eaten alive. Many predators hunt in packs, and their easiest prey are those who stand alone, without a weapon, on a flat area of land where there is little cover. Our ancestors developed a fear response to these situations. "So, despite my 15 years of teaching classes, running workshops, and giving lectures, no matter how comfortable I appear to the audience when at the front of the room, it's a scientific fact that my brain and body will experience some kind of fear before and often while I'm speaking." (Berkun, 2011).

Lesson 6: Give them an outside the box push

When my daughter started middle school, she was very hard on herself and oddly giving up on tasks that may seem too difficult. I'm not sure if the beginning of 6th grade was a whole new adventure to master from 7 different period changes including social skills elective, to her friends and activities—maybe she just ran out of steam.

I started wracking my brain over what would be a great conversation starter. And since I have been getting more active with daily workouts, I figured Nevaeh and I should take a hike. I wanted to see what hills we could climb both literally and figuratively because for one thing, "Mama ain't raising no fool," but most importantly, we are a family that doesn't quit.

So, we took to Elysian Valley Trail in Echo Park on the border of Silver Lake. The trail is a 2.5 to 3-mile loop with slight elevation gain. What I was happy about were the surprise peaks available for climbing if you want to take the road less traveled. Which, I do. Always.

As we started our trail, Nevaeh and I came across a peak that looked a little challenging. And I said, "you know what Nevaeh? I bet you can tackle this peak." She looks nervous for a little bit, and she said, "OK. I'll do it. But mommy, can you come with me?!" You bet I can, kiddo. So, we jog up the peak, and we are both breathing hard at the top. She's smiling so hard, and I can see she's starting to FEEL it. After a quick high-five, we climb down to get back on the dirt path trail.

After we jog for about ten minutes, we came across another peak. This time I encouraged Nevaeh to take it down, solo. The entire time I'm going nuts and cheering her on as she leaps up the hill. Her right foot slipped a little, but she recovered so swiftly it was like nothing happened. (Haha. Take that, therapist who said my kid wouldn't have hand-eye coordination!!)

We set back on the path. About a 30 min trek in we see the steepest hill with loose gravel and some jagged rocks jolting out of the earth. And somewhere in my crazy mind, I say yes. This is the one! Nevaeh and I locked eyes and knew we had to try. And up we went.

Our footing is pretty decent, and we make good progress. We use our upper arm strength to help pull us up the steeper the hill got. Nevaeh and I get to the midway point, and her feet start to slip and mine start to give way too. She yells, "Mommy, I can't do this! I want to go back". And I yell right back, "No! No going back. No quitting. You can do this!" Fear is written all over her little face as I give her a nudge to move forward. She yells, "mom, please?! I can't". And I say, "YOU CAN! Now let's go! Scream if you have to but move now before we both fall!" Nevaeh lets out a warrior cry, digs deep and starts to scramble up the hill. She's moving, and I'm moving right behind her yelling, "you're almost there, almost! Don't give up; keep moving!" And finally, we get to the top of the peak and almost throw ourselves onto the landing. Whew. That was tough.

We get up. Get ourselves together, and I say, "how does it feel not to give up?" She yells, "man! It feels GOOOOODDDDD". And after that there was literally no stopping her, she ran the rest of the course like a machine!

And as she ran, I prayed in gratitude because I know she's got this and then come the unescapable proud mama tears.

Lesson 7: Love unconditionally

"Mommy, I am the shark of the sea. The lion of the land. The eagle of the sky."

"But mommy, I am strong because you are strong."

-Nevaeh, 8

I found myself giving freely of who I was to my daughter without expecting anything in return. In becoming a warrior for my daughter, I also learned that loving someone with a ferociously protective shield came with suffering.

I learned to empathize better by accepting my daughter's feelings while limiting behaviors. Sometimes our children get so caught up in their feelings because they lack the social skills to get what they feel off their chest.

When Nevaeh would become a less outgoing and friendly child, I knew she was becoming a shadow of herself. I could see she often felt misunderstood and out of place. I found ways to better my heart and open wide the opportunity to let her know she was not alone. That often, we all are seeking and searching for our particular tribe of people who understand the essence of who we are as a person.

Positive affirmations are what brought my daughter back from isolation. And repeating those affirmations to Nevaeh allowed the deep of my love to strengthen and grow.

I found my love would prevent me from becoming angry when she lashed out, I was able to: **Listen first, breathe it in, and teach it out.**

The Fight of Your Life

> *"I hated every minute of training, but I said,*
> *'Don't quit. Suffer now and live the rest of*
> *your life as a champion.'"*
>
> -*Muhammad Ali*

Real fighters are cut from a different cloth because very few people have the heart, determination, and mental toughness it takes to succeed. And every real fighter has a reason to fight for whatever it is that they're fighting for.

Your reason, your 'why' is your child.

The well-being of your child will allow you to tap into your reserves when motivation is low. And, you will manage because your 'why' is the strongest one around – the instinct to protect your children.

When I was not around my daughter, I was thinking of ways to improve her heart, charisma, drive, and passion. I thought of ways past the desire to have her socialize and perform academically, but straight into what the core of who my kiddo was. This was me loving my daughter first and autism second.

I fight in every room with every professional who would jump to conclusions first and asks questions later. I believed in myself in any given scenario, it did not matter who they were, what education or title they had. I knew I was stronger, faster, and better than any opponent that would come our way. The commitment it takes for an unshakable belief in your child is as vital as air.

> *"I learned that courage was not the absence of fear, but the triumph over it. The brave man is not he who does not feel afraid, but he who conquers that fear".*
>
> —*Nelson Mandela*

I grew up on an island where we would swim in the ocean's crystal-clear waters. Sometimes we would swim out past the piers to see who was "more fish." One night there was a shark scare, and we were taught if a shark ever came to attack, punch it in the nose. Don't swim away. Summon your strength and punch that shark in the face because facing it was your best bet to stay alive.

To become a better fighter, we have to learn to face our fears and attack it head-on.

The day you received the diagnosis was the day your fight began. You'll have to fight against phrases like, "Oh, if she were normal, it would be easier for you?"

"Are you nervous about having another child? What if she doesn't come out regular?"

Or my personal favorite: "I want you to have another baby, so you can experience what it's like with a great child."

In this fight, we have to give way for other people's misguided information. It will hurt when others use words like *normal, retard, stupid, different, challenged* to describe your child. Deep down, you'll cringe and feel your shoulders hunch, but you're a fighter. You will learn to bob and weave past the words that hurt and the discouragement that tried to knock you down.

Embrace the fighter within. Get to know words that would otherwise harm you for your children's sake. Use the words in your everyday vocabulary if you need to, remove the power and the image they imply and instead, smile because you know they are coming.

Smile because you are almost at the breakthrough point of discovering who you are as a parent. Smile because you're about to unlock the potential in your child. And as all professional fighters know, it's better to stay calm, cool, and collected in a fight for the advantage.

Reject fear.

"Fear is my enemy, my arch nemesis. Fear makes me not want to do homework. Fear tries to take over the city.

The good thing is, I'm a superhero. My game. My rules."

Nevaeh, age 7

This fight comes in so many shapes and forms. To live is to grow and accept the pain that comes with it. Fighters endure unbearable pain that would bring an ordinary person to their knees. And best of all? You will know how to embrace the pain and push through it.

I'm fighting for this life every day. And you should too. Don't give up and don't give in. When the shark of life rears its ugly head, punch that joker in the face.

The Cure to Autism

You know now that autism is a neurodevelopmental disorder, not a mental illness or sickness.

According to the American Psychiatric Association, Mental illnesses are health conditions involving changes in emotion, thinking or behavior (or a combination of these). Mental illnesses are associated with distress and/or problems functioning in social, work or family activities. Mental illness is treatable. The vast majority of individuals with mental illness continue to function in their daily lives. (Parekh, 2018).

Mental illness, affects a person with a previously sane mind as a result of specific events or accidents. (Gupta, 2004). On the other hand, autism is apparent right from the time a child is born.

Prepare yourself now for the assumptions that autism can be cured.

One of the most profoundly disturbing ideas is the agenda from celebrities and pseudoscience filled books suggesting they can cure autism.

There is not a cure from what you know now as a neurodevelopmental disorder. How can you cure a mind that was made that way? What you can do is provide intervention support along with a lot of love towards your children. We have to be careful against this sort of "cure" musing because if we do not, we are opening the door for a child to mimic behavior instead of naturally feeling them or having those abilities.

Nevaeh now no longer meets the eligibility for autism based on markers identified in the DSM5 and psychologist testings. Although I am profoundly in awe of the leaps and bounds my daughter has crossed, in no way am I saying she is cured.

I have found by maintaining this truth and being open with my daughter paved the way for her to flourish beyond measure.

I never wanted Nevaeh to fake how she felt or to imitate those around her to cuddle the feelings of a stranger. Nevaeh never had toy fake a smile during certain moments in the conversation or raise an eyebrow on cue so that others get the impression she was listening.
There is enough space in this beautiful world for all of our children to occupy within the miraculous wonder of their individual truth.

Should you try to cure autism?

No, love your child first. Supply them with the support they need to live a thriving life and never give up on them. If we start declaring that autism spectrum disorder is an epidemic that needs a cure that immediately shifts and contradicts the dialogue of acceptance. If there's any aspect of autism that needs curing, it is the attitude that one can get rid of this condition.

ASD has such a wide range that I understand families who may be frantic to get the best help for their children. The therapy for a person with ASD would be beneficial to anyone. At the end of the day, everyone would be better off with better social skills, behavioral skills, and learning abilities.

Visit my checklist to keep you on the right track.

Think Positively, Change Your Life

For as he thinketh in his heart, so is he

-Proverbs 23:7

I went through a low point when my daughter was six years old. I was not sure how I was going to make it with bills piling up, and not enough money to pay for the therapy Nevaeh needed.

I felt like I was swimming in a pool of decision-making, where every decision had the same high-priority level. Everything felt extraordinarily tough. I was not sure if one choice was the right one or what the outcome would be.

I did learn, however, that the real outcome of executive decision-making is that it changes you to be a more precise thinker. Not only that, when the outcomes from my decision resulted in overwhelmingly positive results, I knew I had the power within to keep moving forward.

I decided to focus my thoughts into healthy ones. Instead of saying, "How am I going to pay this bill?" I would say, "I can't wait to figure this out!" Instead of feeling anxious or worried, I would shout, "I am excited!" Instead of apologizing to someone if I was late, I would say, "thank you for waiting!"

What we think and the way we think about ourselves sets the foundation for the life we will have.

Positive thinking promotes brain growth.

Your thoughts form your character, how you operate in the world, and how far you travel mentally, physically, and spiritually. You are what you think you are because all of your actions started from a thought. Your inner thoughts will always be reflected in your outer circumstances.

Every thought results in the release of brain chemicals. Being focused on negative thoughts effectively drains the brain of its processing and slows down brain function. On the other hand, positive thoughts decrease cortisol (the stress hormone) and produce serotonin (the feel-good hormone), which creates a sense of well-being (Harvard Health Publishing, 2017).

In a study conducted by Barbara Fredrickson, a positive psychology researcher, at the University of North Carolina, participants were broken up into groups and shown different film clips. One group was shown positive emotional clips, and the other was shown clips portraying fear.

Those who watched positive clips demonstrated faster decision-making and a higher range of responses. The other group that was shown negative clips resulted in slower decisions and fewer responses. (Frederickson, 2016).

The results of the study demonstrate that negative thinking can make you see few possibilities and opportunities in life.

Negative thinking only allows you to focus on the situation that is bothering you. It doesn't help you figure out how to get out of the situation. We cannot allow our thoughts to rule us.

Our brains have the incredible ability to reorganize itself by forming new connections between brain cells.

Just as there are multiple ways to drive a road to a destination, there are numerous ways the brain work based on our neuropathways.

The more of a practiced behavior or intentional thought you think, the more you will begin to create a strong neural pathway.

The messages that travel the same pathway in the brain over and over begin to transmit faster and faster. And with enough repetition, behaviors become automatic. Much like riding a bike, we never forget how to carry out these acts. We can change the biological hardwiring of our minds.

The actions we take can literally expand or contract different regions of the brain, firing up circuits or tamping them down.

The more you ask your brain to do, the more cortical space it sets up to handle the new tasks. It responds by forging stronger connections in circuits that underlie the desired behavior or thought and weakening the bonds in others. Thus, what you do and what you think, see, or feel is mirrored in the size of your respective brain regions and the connections your brain forms to accommodate your needs.

This information about the brain is can help you understand ASD. When a person with ASD has difficulty with something, you know that the hard wiring of the brain is positioned differently and more unique.

A unique brain requires a unique way of instructions to modify behaviors.

We speak into the world our desires for our children, and we pray for their hopes and their dreams to not only reveal itself to our kids but to us as well. The diagnosis is no hindrance from our ability to nurture our children.

The idea here is, when it comes to the autism mom, we have found an extraordinary power within ourselves that we did not know we had.

Expect to do better than the world expects of you. Expect to live in a bigger world than the one you see. Recognize that being true to yourself is not the same as being true to a label.

By reducing your self-limiting beliefs, you will effectively release your brakes and experience growth like you never imagined. Essentially, you can change your entire life simply by harnessing the power of positive thinking.

> *"The future belongs to those who believe in the beauty of their dreams."*
>
> - *Eleanor Roosevelt*

Most people want to obtain their goals but they get in their own way by not having the confidence in themselves. Everything that we have ever hoped to achieve has been so intricately placed inside of us.

Once we start trusting ourselves, wonderful things happen. We see opportunity making a way for itself. We become more productive, happy, and in tuned with our surrounding. We can close the deal and get any job done.

We have to be careful that, in our willingness to take care of our family, this same desire does not spill over into areas that do not deserve our devotion. In pleasing others, outside of our family, we tend to look for someone to validate us. It is very easy to become a people-pleaser given the route of excuses we have had to make for our children in school and social settings.

You will need to come back into yourself and snatch your confidence back. It is okay to choose you and not the nice version of you. I have found that nice people are looking for acceptance and validation, so they turn into people pleasers or pushovers all in the hopes that they have made someone happy.

I will let you in on a little secret, there is a difference between nice and kind. And contrary to popular belief, I am not nice. I am kind. I set boundaries. I am vocal about my limits. I am devoted. Loyal.

My kindness comes from a place of confidence and a genuine concern for outcomes.

> *A tulip does not strive to impress anyone. It doesn't struggle to be different than a rose — there is room in the garden for every flower.*
>
> *— Author Unknown*

Don't try to impress the people you cannot lean on and focus on your fragrance. Because the more you make the right decisions aligned with your deepest desires and your core values, the faster you will reach your goals.

My Gift to You

To every person who has taken the time to read, reread, make notations, rip pages out and paste on the wall – I am with you. My knowledge and confidence, I give to you.

I battle alongside those of you who know you can change the trajectory for your life if you just believe. D.H. Lawrence wrote, "I never saw a wild thing sorry for itself. A small bird will drop frozen dead from a bough without ever having felt sorry for itself." You no longer feel sorry for yourself.

Your development will be met with dignity at all times.

There are no shortcuts to destiny. Sometimes you have to remind yourself of where have been so you can appreciate where you're going. I want to remind you who you are.

You did not study hard, put in the extra time at work, give up your free time or and sacrifice beyond for nothing.

Every decision you make to better yourself and your child is a purposed stepping stone in the pursuit of a life you deserve to live.

You will walk and not grow weary, run and not faint.

You are will do a better job raising loving, wholesome, thriving children while still living your own *happie life.*

I encourage you to say, "thank you," in advance, because success is already yours.

Checklist for Success

☐ **Make it up in your mind that you're not at fault for the diagnosis of autism spectrum disorder therefore, you are not intimidated.**

Do not let all the doctors, therapists, educators, or the price tag that comes with autism sway your confidence. You can master it all.

☐ **Do not even think about feeling sorry for yourself.**

I encourage you to seek out help and often. Jot down in a diary your feelings so you can get those out and stay focused. Your role as your child's advocate is going to keep you busy. Things are going to be okay.

☐ **Don't feel sorry for your child.**

Your child is still your child, a perfect and healthy, amazing child that you first fell in love with. Keep that love, respect that love.

□ **You will need to assemble a tribe and be on the lookout for when they show themselves.**

Call your tribe and assign some tasks to them to help you with your daily life. Assign small things like help on a grocery run or find a companion to take a walk with you. These small acts of support can really help you manage your day-to-day life.

□ **Get support for yourself.**

Joining a parent support group or chatting with other parents who have kids with special needs can be a relief.

Many communities also have volunteer advocates and professional advocates who can explain the law to you and go with you to meetings to make sure you get heard and that the school responds as it should.

☐ Know your child's rights.

It's vital to be up to date with your state's education laws and the policies of the local school system. You will be taken more seriously by administrators if you have taken the time to learn and understand what you have to work with.

☐ Contact your Regional Center or third party support/diagnostic center for an Independent Educational Evaluation.

You have the right to have your child evaluated independently. This means you have the right to have your child evaluated by someone other than the staff who work for the school system. The purpose of the evaluation is to see if your child meets the eligibility for autism and what, if any, special needs they have.

When Nevaeh was first diagnosed over seven years ago, a lot of programs were not available. Programs that were available cost so much money that I could not even imagine affording them. Having the support of an organization that contracts with the Department of Developmental Services to provide or coordinate services and supports for individuals with developmental disabilities is invaluable.

Once you receive this evaluation the third-party center will most likely refer you to free services within your county and they will help keep up with the progress of your child annually.

□ **After you have received your IEE, if you have not done so already, request for an Individualized Education Plan from your school.**

An IEP is more than just a written legal document (or "plan"). It's a map that lays out the program of special education instruction and services kids need to make progress and succeed in school.

Each program is designed to meet a child's exact needs. The term IEP is also used to refer to the written plan that spells out the specific types of help the child will get.

The IEP process begins with a full evaluation that shows your child's strengths and weaknesses. The results allow you and the school to create a program of services and supports tailored to meet your child's needs.

With an IEP, your child will get individualized instruction that focuses on improving specific skills. But there are other types of help that can also be included in an IEP.

You might be able to ensure extended time on tests or assistive technology in the classroom. Your IEP is a state- and federally protected contract that ensures the rights of your child.

If you can find the harmony between your goal for your child and school personnel professional expertise, you child will win in every area with support, guidance and goals.

□ **Submit the Independent Educational Evaluation to your school.**

As your child's school conducts their evaluation for the Individualized Education Plan, submitting your IEE will come in handy during the IEP process in case you have a question or do not necessarily agree with their evaluations.

□ **Get on board with the school.**

A little understanding goes a long way. Schools are straining to stay within budgets and to stretch their money the best they can. Yes, we all understand that. But when it's our child who is suffering or whose scholarship is falling behind, it's hard to stay sympathetic. (Hartwell-Walker, 2018).
Services for one child can mean that 20 other kids are in an overcrowded classroom. We do have to advocate well for our children, but it helps us be more collaborative when we can also appreciate the position it puts school officials in.

□ Always prepare for meetings at school.

Take a list of talking points and questions. Your time and the time of the people you are meeting with is valuable.

□ When you can, always take your partner or a friend with you to meetings.

Often there are six or more professionals around the table, and it feels like the world is against you. If you cannot hold your own, have an ally with you. And, shameless plug here, be sure to take my book with you: *IEP Parent Survival Guide*.

□ Keep your cool.

Be assertive but submit requests in kindness. Laugh off what is bothering you and stay focused on your agenda.

□ **Consider your options for Social Security Benefits.**

If your child or a loved one's child has autism, they could be eligible for payments from the Social Security Administration in the form of monthly payments. Your payment eligibility depends on your resources and areas of need and can be anywhere from $300-$700 a month.

□ **Seek out a speech therapist.**

People with ASD may face difficulties with speech and pronunciation. Using speech therapy can greatly

address these conditions so that these individuals can learn how to voice themselves better.

□ **Seek out an occupational therapist.**

An occupational therapist will help with fine motor skills and hand-eye coordination.

Some sessions of OT could also consist of hygiene skills and independence lessons which can help train your child to be self-sufficient.

□ Consider relationship-based training.

Relationship-based approach ensures that the individual learns how to be sensitive towards other people and their needs just how anyone else would.

This will also help with social skills, how to properly express feelings, boundaries and limitations between one's peer group.

Your school might also offer a social-skills elective specific for children with autism.

□ Consider sensory integration.

Such people may not be able to understand concepts like depth, balance, width, and other forms of senses that are quite crucial for daily activities.

This sort of therapeutic activity along with occupational therapy could benefit your child in an enormous way.

□ **Whichever type of therapy you decide best meets the need for your child, get to know your child's speech, occupational, and/or motor skills therapist.**

Constant communication, clarity on goals and sharing your child's IEP will help everyone stay on track. They are all such an intricate part in the life of your child.

Fun story: Nevaeh tried to hustle her speech therapist out of a dollar.

During the session, he'll say words wrong on purpose, and when she does, she has to "pay him with repeating the right words." So, she said "Hey, Mr. Gomez, so when you say a wrong word can you pay me a dollar?

The relationship Nevaeh developed with her speech therapist was fun and amazing to see.

□ Avoid frivolous debates. Use your time and energy wisely.

Don't get caught up in the autism community debates that lead to nowhere. You can decide to disclose your child's diagnosis to everyone in your community or keep it in your house.

Prior to making our blog and the road to writing this book, Nevaeh and I had very real and honest conversations – she wanted to inspire those on the spectrum and I wanted to inspire parents to advocate for their children.

☐ **Make a wish list on Amazon and start compiling sensory-safe toys tactile manipulatives, study stress balls, and other tactile toys.**

This will help you to keep track of the items you want and budget them properly.

☐ **Be on the look-out for clothing for your kiddos.**

Children with autism are sensitive to textures so try to find tagless clothing, 100% cotton, fully breathable, pull on pants, long sleeve shirts and fixed pants. The last thing you want your child to have to tug on their clothing or stretch incessantly because of irritants.

I see you

I can imagine what you are feeling. I have been there.

Although this book is mainly written for the autism mom, I hope that fathers, aunts or uncles, foster parents or adoptive parents, friends, cousins, administrators—anyone reading this will now have a better grasp on the life of autism, from the lens of a single parent, on how to support and advocate for your loved ones.

Nevaeh and I conquered many obstacles since the time of diagnosis until now. Being overcomers have brought Nevaeh and I closer than I ever thought possible.

And because I believe in ending things the way they began, here is what I want you to do.

I want you to breathe in.

Hold that air. And exhale out.

Feel your strength coming back to you.

Breathe in again.

Feel peace surround you.

Breathe in. Hold it. And exhale out.

You are bold.

You are rebellious.

You are armed with information.

There is nothing you cannot do.

And most importantly, you've got work to do.

God bless you and your family.

Glossary

The following are commonly used definitions in the world of ASD that you should get to learn. These terms were pulled from a variety of resources.

AAC: Assistive Augmentative Communications – A Speech-Language Therapists' term for communication using a picture board or recorded messages activated by buttons, etc.

ABA: Applied Behavior Analysis – A method of teaching designed to analyze and change behavior in a precisely measurable and accountable manner. Also called behavior modification. Skills are broken down into their simplest components and then taught to the child through a system of reinforcement.

ABC: Autism Behavior Checklist – A diagnostic device for autism. A checklist containing a list of behaviors and weighted scores which appear to be capable of measuring the level of autistic behaviors in individuals.

Abstract Thinking – Deductive thinking, not concrete and singles out the rational, logical qualities.

ACCESS – Identification card issued to Medial Assistance recipients; used by Medical Assistance providers to verify client eligibility.

ADA: Americans with Disabilities Act – A civil rights law passed in 1990 that does not allow discrimination against people with disabilities in employment, public service, and public accommodations.

Adaptive Skills (Functional Skills) – Those used in daily living such as eating, dressing and toileting. Self-Help Skills.

ADD: Attention Deficit Disorder – A syndrome exhibited usually by children aged seven years and below. The disorder is characterized by the child's persistent impulsiveness, hyperactivity and very short attention span.

Advocate/Advocacy – Someone who takes action to help someone else (as in "educational advocate"); also, to take action on someone's behalf assuring services, appropriate for you and your child, are received.

AIT: Auditory Integration Training – Developed by Dr. Guy Bernard, an Ear, Nose and Throat physician, to rehabilitate disorders of the auditory system, such as hearing loss.

ALD: Assistive Listing Device – Any type of device that can help you function better in your day-to-day communication situations.

Aphasia – Loss of ability to use or understand words.

Apraxia – A disorder of voluntary movement, consisting of partial or total incapacity to execute purposeful movements, without impairment of muscular power, sensibility and coordination. The person has difficulty sequencing movements in the service of a goal. May be specific to speech.

AS: Asperger's Syndrome – A developmental disorder on the autism spectrum defined by impairments in communications and social development and by repetitive interests and behaviors. Unlike typical autism, individuals with Asperser's Syndrome have no significant delay in language and cognitive development.

ASA: Autism Society of America – A voice and resource of the entire autism community in education, advocacy, services, research and support. The ASA is committed to meaningful participation and self-determination in all aspects of life for individuals on the autism spectrum and their families. ASA accomplishes its ongoing mission through close collaboration with a successful network of chapters, members and supporters.

ASD: Autism Spectrum Disorder – Term that encompasses autism and similar disorders. More specifically, the following five disorders listed in DSM-IV: Autistic Disorder, Asperger's Disorder, PDD-NOS, Childhood Disintegrative Disorder, and Rett's Disorder.

Assessment – A collection of information about a child's needs, which may include social, psychological, and educational evaluations used to determine services.

Assistive Technology – A generic term that includes assistive, adaptive, and rehabilitative devices and the process used in selecting, locating, and using them. AT promotes greater independence for people with disabilities by enabling them to perform tasks that they were formerly unable to accomplish, or had great difficulty accomplishing, by providing enhancements to or changed methods of interacting with the technology needed to accomplish such tasks.

Auditory Processing – The ability to understand and use information that is heard, both words as well as other nonverbal sounds. Augmentative Communication – Special devise that provides an alternative for spoken language. For example, photographs and picture exchange communication.

Autism – A disability characterized by severe language and communication deficits, lack of normal relatedness, bizarre movement and self-stimulatory patterns, lack of normal handling of toys and other objects, and lack of most normal functional skills. Life Long developmental disability, neurological disorder affecting brain function.

Baseline – The current level the child is functioning at before instruction.

Bayley Scales – A developmental assessment used for children age one month to 3 1/2 years old. It is comprised of a mental, motor and behavior scale. This scale has a mean of 100 and a standard deviation of 15.

BHRS: Behavioral Health Rehabilitation Services – Community-based mental health treatment available to children with mental health needs in Pennsylvania.

BSC: Behavior Specialist Consultant – Assists design, goals, techniques & implantation of behavior management plan through a wraparound provider.

BSE: Bureau of Special Education – Part of the Pennsylvania Department of Education that oversees all matters concerning special education.

BSP: Behavior Support Plan/BIP: Behavior Intervention Plan – Multi-component behavior intervention plans, with multiple layers of support, are in fact the best way to establish effective and comprehensive strategies for addressing challenging behavior. All interventions should be selected based on the results of the Functional Behavioral Assessment and intervention, designed to promote the acquisition of new skills and to decrease problem behaviors.

BSU: Base Service Unit – A component of the county's Mental Health system that provides services to eligible county residents.

CADDRE: Center for Autism & Developmental Disabilities Research & Epidemiology –The Children's Health Act of 2000 directed the Center for Disease Control and Prevention (CDC) to establish regional centers of excellence for autism spectrum disorders (ASD) and other developmental disabilities. These centers make up the Centers for Autism and Developmental Disabilities Research and Epidemiology (CADDRE) Network. The CADDRE Network is currently working on the Study to

Explore Early Development (SEED) – A five-year, multi-site collaborative study to help identify factors that may put children at risk for autism spectrum disorders (ASD).

CAN: Cure Autism Now – An organization of parents, clinicians and leading scientists committed to accelerating the pace of biomedical research in autism through raising money for research projects, education and outreach. The organization's primary focus is to fund essential research through a variety of programs designed to encourage innovative approaches toward identifying the causes, prevention, treatment and a cure for autism and related disorders.

Childhood Autism Rating Scale – A test developed at TEACCH to diagnose autism. The child is rated in 15 areas on a scale up to 4 yielding a total up to 60, ranges are considered to be non-autistic, autistic, and severely autistic.

CBCL: Achenbach Child Behavior Checklist – A diagnostic instruments can be used to develop behavior profiles and record individual competencies and problems. The instruments yield scores related to: Total Problem & Total Competence as well as broad-banding Internalizing, and Externalizing problem scales, and competence scores on Social, Activities and School subscales. In addition, eight or nine behavior problem scales, called Syndromes are identified, the number and definition of which vary for the age/gender groups).

CHAT: Checklist for Autism in Toddlers – A checklist to be used by General Practitioners at 18 months to see if a child has Autism Spectrum Disorder. Described in Baron-Cohen S; Allen J: Gillberg C. "Can autism be detected at 18 months? The needle, the haystack, and the CHAT." British Journal of Psychiatry, 1992 Dec, 161:839043 (UI: 93130306)

Cognitive – A term that describes the process people use for remembering, reasoning, understanding, and using judgment: in special education terms, a cognitive disability refers to difficulty in learning. Skills that involve problem solving and the ability to classify, retain and recall information on a short and long-term basis.

Community-Based – Instruction occurs in natural environment instead of school campus.

DAN: Defeat Autism Now – Dedicated to educating parents and clinicians regarding biomedical-based research, appropriate testing and safe and effective interventions for autism.

DD: Developmental Delay – A child who acquires skills after the expected age in achieving cognitive, adaptive, physical, communication and social skills.

DIBELS: Dynamic Indicators of Basic Early Literacy Skills – Are a set of standardized, individually administered measures of early literacy development. They are designed to be short (one minute) fluency measures used to regularly monitor the development of pre-reading and early reading skills.

DSM-IV: Diagnostic and Statistical Manual, 4th Edition – A manual published by the American Psychiatric Association (APA) which describes all of the diagnostic criteria and the systematic descriptions of various mental disorders.

Discrete Trail Therapy – This is a specific method of instruction in which a task is isolated and taught one-on one by repeatedly presenting the same task. Responses are recorded, mastered and then acquired as a new task. The term is also often used in a fewer specific ways, as a synonym for ABA.

Due Process Hearing – Held in the same way as a trial at the courthouse. The parties present evidence to the Hearing Officer who acts as both judge and jury. The purpose of this due process is to resolve disagreements between families and a regional center and/or local education agency (LEA) related to a proposal or refusal for identification, evaluation, assessment, placement, or services.

Dyslexia – Learning disability affecting reading ability. Persons with dyslexia may have difficulty remembering, recognizing, and or reversing written letters, numbers, and words, might read backwards, and have poor handwriting.

Dyspraxia – Term for a neurological symptom; a problem with "praxis", i.e. planning, initiating, sequencing, and carrying out volitional movements. I think "dyspraxia"" and "apraxia" mean the same thing having been coined in different professional circles. See the variants of apraxia and dyspraxia.

Early Intervention Services – Applies to children before the age of three who are discovered to have or be at risk of developing a handicapping condition or other special need that may affect their development (physical, cognitive, communication, social development). Early intervention consists in the provision of services such children and their families for the purpose of lessening the effects of the condition.

Echolalia – Repeating back something said to you. Delayed Echolalia is repeating it later. Both behaviors are found in many autistics. Functional echolalia is using a quoted phrase in a way that has shared meaning, for example, a child who sings the Barney jingle to ask for a Barney videotape, or says "Get your shoes and socks" to ask to go outside.

EEG – Electroencephalogram – a graphic record of the brain's electrical activity.

EPSDT: Early Periodic Screening Diagnosis and Treatment – Is the child health component of Medicaid. It's required in every state and is designed to improve the health of low-income children, by financing appropriate and necessary pediatric services. It is designed to identifying problems early, starting at birth, checking children's health at periodic/age-appropriate intervals, do physical, mental, developmental, dental, hearing, vision, and other screening tests to detect potential problems, performing diagnostic tests to follow up when a risk is identified, and treating the problems found.

ESY: Extended School Year – Services provided during times when school is closed as in the case of summer break.

Expressive Language Disorder - Developmental expressive language disorder in which a child has lower-than normal proficiency in vocabulary, the production of complex sentences, and recall of words. Child will typically use gestures, words, and written symbols to communicate.

Facilitated Communications – The facilitators make physical contact with the arm or wrist of the disabled person and the user is said to communicate by pointing toward a communication device (often a picture board, speech synthesizer or keyboard) by their own will.

FAPE: Free Appropriate Public Education Fine Motor – Relating to the use of the small muscles of the body, such as those of the hands, feet, fingers and toes.

Fragile X Syndrome – A genetic condition in which one part of the X-chromosome has a defect. The condition causes mental retardation.

GARS: Gilliam Autism Rating Scale – Is a developmental checklist to assist in the identification of persons who are autistic. The easy format of the test allows teachers, parents, or others who have knowledge of the subject's behavior to complete it. There are fourteen items in each of the four subtests: 1) Stereotyped Behavior; 2) Communication; 3) Social Interactions; and 4) Developmental Disturbances.

GF/CF: Gluten-Free/Casein-Free – Referring to a diet which restricts the intake of Gluten.

HFA: High-Functioning Autistic or High-Functioning Autism – Refers to the cognitive abilities of a person with autism

HIPAA: Health Insurance Portability and Accountability Act – The federal law which insures comprehensive protection for the privacy of personal health information.

Hyperlexia – A condition in which the main characteristics are an above average ability to read accompanied with a blow average ability to understand spoken language.

Hypersensitivity – Being overly sensitive to touch, movement, sights, or sounds.

Hyposensitivity – Being under responsive to touch, movement, sights, or sounds.

IDEA: Individuals with Disabilities Education Act – Federal legislation (Public Law 105-17) passed in 1997 as a reauthorization of the Education of the Handicapped Act (EHA) passed in 1975. Provides mandate and some funding for certain services for students who have disabilities.

IEP: Individualized Education Plan – A yearly education plan written by teachers, therapists, psychologists, etc. and the child's parents for school age children with disabilities for someone who needs special education. The IEP addresses the student's needs and the educational supports and services required to meet those needs.

IFSP: Individualized Family Service Plan – An education plan written by teachers, therapists, psychologists, etc. and the child's parents for a child with disabilities. The plan runs from birth to 2 years old.

Inclusion – Disabled children receive services in their home school and are placed in the same classroom with nonhandicapped children. The practice of educating all or most children in the same classroom, including children with physical, mental, and developmental disabilities. Inclusion classes often require a special assistant to the classroom teacher.

Interdisciplinary Team – Various Individuals from different disciplines that assess children's needs (speech therapist, occupational therapist, nurse, psychologist, etc.)

IU: Intermediate Unit – United States regional educational service agencies, established by the Pennsylvania General Assembly. Intermediate Units serve a given geographic area's educational needs and function as a step of organization above that of a public school district, but below that of the Pennsylvania Department of Education. There are twenty-nine intermediate units in the Commonwealth of Pennsylvania, each serving a given region.

LEA: Local Educational Agency – The educational agency that has the financial obligation to see that for each student for which it is responsible receives FAPE.

Learning Disability – A child with average or above average potential has difficulty learning in one or more areas (such as reading or math) and exhibits a severe discrepancy between their ability and achievement.

Performance Scale – A nonverbal assessment of intelligence, used primarily with children with communication difficulties. It gives both an IQ score, and an age equivalent for the child's level of functioning.

LRE: Least Restrictive Environment – A child should be educated in the least restrictive environment for his or her disability and which meets his or her needs. An educational setting which gives students with disabilities a place to learn to the best of their ability and also have contact with children without disabilities.

MA: Medical Assistance/Medicaid – A public insurance system that provides free health insurance to persons who are eligible. It is jointly funded by the federal and state governments and administered by state governments. It is not "welfare" and does not provide its beneficiaries with cash assistance.

Mainstreaming – Placement of a disabled child with non-disabled peers in a regular classroom, some or all of the child's day is spent in a regular classroom.

Mediation – A free dispute resolution process available to parents of children with disabilities. If you are in disagreement with the school district, you can ask for mediation. A third-party mediator will be assigned to try and help resolve the issues.

MR: Mental Retardation – Is a disability characterized by significant limitations both in intellectual functioning and in adaptive behavior as expressed in conceptual, social, and practical adaptive skills.

MRI: Magnetic Resonance Imaging – Using very powerful magnetic waves to create images.

MT: Mobile Therapist or Mobile Therapy – Refers to therapy services available through BHRS.

Neurologist – A physician specialized in medical problems associated with the brain and spinal cord.

Neurotypical (NT) – Is a neologism used to describe people whose neurological development and state are consistent with what most people would perceive as normal in their ability to process linguistic information and social cues. While originally coined among the autistic community as a label for non-autistic persons, the concept was later adopted by both the neurodiversity movement and the scientific community.

NOREP: Notice of Recommended Educational Placement – A form filled out by the school district or other educational entity which describes a child recommended placement. In theory, it reviews the learner's needs and strengths, describes other settings that were considered, and explains why other options were rejected. It's important to note that the NOREP should be developed in cooperation with other members of the IEP (Individualized Educational Program) team.

OCD: Obsessive Compulsive Disorder – Classified in DSM-IV as an anxiety disorder, OCD characterized by recurrent, time-consuming obsessive or compulsive behaviors that cause distress and/or impairment. The obsessions may be repetitive intrusive images, thoughts, or impulses. Often the compulsive behaviors, such as hand-washing or cleaning rituals, are an attempt to displace the obsessive thoughts (DSM-IV).

OCR: Office for Civil Rights – Exists to ensure equal access to education and to promote educational excellence throughout the nation through vigorous enforcement of civil rights. OCR serves student populations facing discrimination and the advocates and institutions promoting systemic solutions to civil rights problems. An important responsibility is resolving complaints of discrimination.

ODD: Oppositional Defiant Disorder – A psychiatric behavior disorder that is characterized by aggressiveness and a tendency to purposefully bother and irritate others as a recurrent pattern of negativistic, defiant, disobedient, and hostile behavior that persists for at least six months. Behaviors included the following: losing one's temper; arguing with adults; actively defying requests; refusing to follow rules; deliberately annoying other people; blaming others for one's own mistakes or misbehavior; being touchy, easily annoyed or angered, resentful, spiteful, or vindictive. These behaviors cause significant difficulties with family and friends and at school or work.

ODR: Office for Dispute Resolution – Provides the resources for parents and educational agencies to resolve disputes concerning the identification, evaluation, educational placement, or the provision of a free appropriate public education for students with disabilities, students who are gifted and children with disabilities served by the early intervention system.

OI: Orthopedic Impairment – Orthopedic impairment refers to students whose severe orthopedic impairments affect their education performance to the degree that the student requires special education. Includes impairment cause by congenital anomalies.

Oral Motor – Relating to the movement of the muscles in and around the mouth.

OT: Occupational Therapy or Occupational Therapist – A therapist that focuses on daily living skills, sensory integration, self-help skills, playing, adaptive behavior and fine motor skills. An Occupational Therapist provides Sensory Integration Therapy.

PDD: Pervasive Developmental Disorder – A group of developmental disabilities which are neurological and usually of an unknown origin. Characteristics include reduced ability to understand language, communicate, and interact with others, and a limited variety of activities and interests. Types of pervasive development disorder include autism, Rett's Syndrome, Heller's Syndrome, and Asperger's Syndrome.

PDD-NOS: Pervasive Developmental Disorder Not Otherwise Specified – A 'sub threshold' condition in which some – but not all – features of autism or another explicitly identified Pervasive Developmental Disorder are identified. PDD-NOS is often incorrectly referred to as simply "PDD." The term PDD refers to the class of conditions to which autism belongs. PDD is NOT itself a diagnosis, while PDD-NOS IS a diagnosis. The term Pervasive Developmental Disorder – Not Otherwise Specified (PDD-NOS; also referred to as "atypical personality development," "atypical PDD," or "atypical autism") is included in DSM-IV to encompass cases where there is marked impairment of social interaction, communication, and/or stereotyped behavior patterns or interest, but when full features for autism or another explicitly defined PDD are not met.

PECS: Picture Exchange Communication System – Is an augmentative communication system developed to help individuals quickly acquire a functional means of communication (Bondy and Frost, 1994). PECS is appropriate for individuals who do not use speech or who may speak with limited effectiveness: those who have articulation or motor planning difficulties, limited communicative partners, lack of initiative in communication.

Pica – Ingestion of nonfood items (crayons, paint chips, etc.)

PT: Physical Therapy/Therapist – Provides evaluation and treatment of physical disabilities to help the person improve the used of bones, muscles, joints, and nerves through exercise and massage.

PUNS: Prioritization of Urgency of Needs for Services – Provides a uniform instrument that is used by County Mental Retardation Programs, on an on-going basis, to collect a standard set of data on individuals who are waiting for mental retardation services and supports. It is a significant management tool for County Mental Retardation Programs. PUNS has been formally adopted by the Office of Mental Retardation as a requirement for annual County Plans and for use in program budgeting.

RAST: Regional Assessment and Support Team – A team comprised of certified special education staff and a school psychologist or contracted specialists. The teams are coordinated by the Pennsylvania Department of Education, Bureau of Special Education. Each correctional institution is supported by one of the three Regional Assessment and Support Teams, which provide technical assistance, in-service training, related services, compliance monitoring of correctional institutions, and psychological assessments as needed.

Receptive Language – Is the input system of language. It is what we see and hear and the information that we take in. Receptive language is the comprehension of information. Language does not improve according to age alone – it develops as one skill helps the next. Once an early skill develops, it allows more difficult skills to be learned. Language develops in a way similar to physical or movement skills: One stage leads to the next. Receptive language skills begin as early as birth and get stronger with each stage in development.

Receptive Language Disorder – A disorder where the child has difficulties with understanding what is said to them. The symptoms vary between individuals but, generally, problems with language comprehension usually begin before the age of four years. Children need to understand language before they can use language effectively. In most cases, the child with a receptive language problem also has an expressive language disorder, which means they have trouble using spoken language. Other names for receptive language disorder include central auditory processing disorder and comprehension deficit. Treatment options include speech–language therapy.

Reinforcement – Providing a pleasant consequence (positive reinforcement) or removing an unpleasant consequence (negative reinforcement) after a behavior in order to increase or maintain that behavior.

Related Services – Other support services that a child with disabilities requires such as transportation, occupational, physical and speech pathology services, interpreters, and medical services.

Respite Care – Skilled adult or child care and supervision that can be provided in your home or the home of a care provider. Respite care may be available for several hours per week or for overnight stays.

Reverse Mainstreaming – When non-disabled children go to the special education classroom to play and learn with children who are disabled.

RTF: Residential Treatment Facilities –Both facilities that are accredited by Joint Commission on the Accreditation of HealthCare Facilities (JCAHO) and those that are licensed and supervised by the Department of Public Welfare but are not JCAHO-accredited.

Section 504 – Civil rights statute, disabled child receives accommodations & modifications in a formal, written service plan, not an IEP.

Self-Stimulatory Behavior – A term for behaviors whose primary purpose appears to be to stimulate one's own senses. An example is rocking one's body: Many people with autism report that some "self stims" may serve a regulatory function for them.

Sensor Motor – Pertaining to brain activity other than automatic functions (respiration, circulation, sleep) or cognition. Sensor motor activity includes voluntary movement and senses like sight touch and hearing.

SI: Sensory Integration – The ability to take in information through the senses of touch, movement, smell, taste, vision, and hearing, and to combine the resulting perceptions with prior information, memories, and knowledge already stored in the brain, in order to derive coherent meaning from processing the stimuli. The mid-brain and brainstem regions of the central nervous system are early centers in the processing pathway for sensory integration. These brain regions are involved in processes including coordination, attention, arousal, and autonomic function. After sensory information passes through these centers, it is then routed to brain regions responsible for emotions, memory, and higher-level cognitive functions.

SID: Sensory Integration Dysfunction – Also called sensory processing disorder, it is a neurological disorder causing difficulties with processing information from the five classic senses (vision, auditory, touch, olfaction, and taste), the sense of movement (vestibular system), and/or the positional sense (proprioception). Sensory information is sensed normally, but perceived abnormally.

SLP or S-LP: Speech-Language Pathologist – A qualified person who improves and/or corrects communication problems.

Social Skills – Positive, appropriate, social behaviors, needed to communicate and interact.

Speech Therapy – Professional who is qualified to diagnose and treat speech, language & voice disorders.

Splinter Skills – A specific skill a child may do exceptional well despite lower scores in other areas.

Theory of Mind – Is a specific cognitive ability to understand others or interpret their minds. It is something that all people must develop in order to understand the minds of other people.

TSS: Therapeutic Staff Support – Supervised by BSC--provide direct interventions, structure activities for child and assist in development of appropriate skills.

Vineland Adaptive Behavior Scales – An assessment measure sometimes used to evaluate a child's functioning in social, communication, behavioral, and self-help areas.

WISC-IV: Wechsler Intelligence Scale for Children – An individually administered clinical instrument for assessing the intellectual functioning of children.

Wraparound – A behavioral health rehabilitation services process that provides individualized, comprehensive, community-based services and supports to children and adolescents with serious emotional and/or behavioral disturbances so they can be reunited and/or remain with their families and communities.

References

Baio J, W. L. (2018). Prevalence of Autism Spectrum Disorder
    Among Children Aged 8 Years — Autism and Developmental
    Disabilities Monitoring Network, 11 Sites, United States, 2014.
    MMWR Surveill Summ.

Berkun, S. (2011). Confessions of a public speaker. Farnham:
    O Reilly.

Bird, G., & Cook, R. (2013). Mixed emotions: The contribution of
    alexithymia to the emotional symptoms of autism. Translational
    Psychiatry. https://doi.org/10.1038/tp.2013.61

Bitsika, V., & Sharpley, C. F. (2016). Which Aspects of
    Challenging Behaviour Are Associated with Anxiety across two
    Age Groups of Young Males with an Autism Spectrum
    Disorder? Journal of Developmental and Physical Disabilities,
    28(5), 685–701. https://doi.org/10.1007/s10882-016-9502-4

Bölte, S., Bartl-Pokorny, K. D., Jonsson, U., Berggren, S.,
    Zhang, D., Kostrzewa, E., ... Marschik, P. B. (2016). How can
    clinicians detect and treat autism early? Methodological trends
    of technology use in research. Acta Paediatrica, International
    Journal of Paediatrics. https://doi.org/10.1111/apa.13243

Dawson, G. (2008). Early behavioral intervention, brain
    plasticity, and the prevention of autism spectrum disorder.
    Development and Psychopathology.
    https://doi.org/10.1017/S0954579408000370

Diagnostic and statistical manual of mental disorders (5th ed.).
    (2013). American Psychiatric Association.

Elliot, A., Fairchild, M. & Franklin A. (2014) Handbook of Color
    Psychology. (Cambridge Handbooks in Psychology) 1st Edition

el Kaliouby, R., Picard, R., & Baron-Cohen, S. (2006). Affective
    computing and autism. Annals of the New York Academy of
    Sciences. https://doi.org/10.1196/annals.1382.016

Gupta, Vidya Bhushan. Complementary and Alternative
    Medicine. New York Medical College and Columbia University,
    2004. Pediatric Habilitation, Volume 12.

Handleman, J.S., Harris, S., eds. Preschool Education
    Programs for Children with Autism (2nd ed). Austin, TX: Pro-
    Ed. 2000.

Hartwell-Walker, M. (2018). Advocating for Your Child within
    theSchool System. Psych Central. Retrieved on May 22, 2019,
    from https://psychcentral.com/lib/advocating-for-your-child-
    within-the-school-system/

Harvard Health Publishing (2015) How Depression Affects Your
     Thinking Skills https://www.health.harvard.edu/
     depression/how-depression-affects-your-thinking-skills
Helen Tager-Flusberg. (n.d.). Brain Imaging Studies in Autism
     Spectrum Disorders. Retrieved April 22, 2019, from
     https://www.aane.org/brain-imaging-studies-autism-spectrum-
     disorders
Kalat, J. W. (2016). Biological psychology (12e.). Boston, MA:
     Cengage Learning.
Kim HJ Cho MH et al: Deficient autophagy in microglia impairs
     synaptic pruning and causes social behavioral defects. Mol
     Psychiatry. 2017 Nov;22(11):1576-1584. doi:
     10.1038/mp.2016.103. Epub 2016 Jul 12.
Lange, Nicholas & Travers, Brittany & D. Bigler, Erin & Prigge,
     Molly & L. Froehlich, Alyson & Nielsen, Jared & Cariello,
     Annahir & A. Zielinski, Brandon & Anderson, Jeffrey & Thomas
     Fletcher, P & A. Alexander, Andrew & Lainhart, Janet. (2014).
     Longitudinal Volumetric Brain Changes in Autism Spectrum
     Disorder Ages 6–35 Years. Autism Research. 8.
     10.1002/aur.1427.
Levy, S. Complementary and Alternative Medicine Among
     Children Recently Diagnosed with Autistic Spectrum Disorder;
     Journal of Developmental and Behavioral Pediatrics,
     December 2003; vol 24: pp 418-423. News release, Health
     Behavior News Service.
Merin, N., Young, G. S., Ozonoff, S., & Rogers, S. J. (2007).
     Visual Parekh fixation patterns during reciprocal social
     interaction distinguish a subgroup of 6-month-old infants at-risk
     for autism from comparison infants. Journal of Autism and
     Developmental Disorders. https://doi.org/10.1007/s10803-006-
     0342-4
Min, C. H., & Tewfik, A. H. (2010). Automatic characterization
     and detection of behavioral patterns using linear predictive
     coding of accelerometer sensor data. In 2010 Annual
     International Conference of the IEEE Engineering in Medicine
     and Biology Society, EMBC'10.
     https://doi.org/10.1109/IEMBS.2010.5627850
Morales, M., Mundy, P., Delgado, C. E. F., Yale, M., Messinger,
     D., Neal, R., & Schwartz, H. K. (2000). Responding to Joint
     Attention Across the 6- Through 24-Month Age Period and
     Early Language Acquisition. Journal of Applied Developmental
     Psychology. https://doi.org/10.1016/S0193-3973(99)00040-4

National Research Council. Educating Children with Autism. Washington, DC: National Academy Press, 2001., R., M.D., M.P.H. (2018). Mental Illness. Retrieved 2018, from https://www.psychiatry.org/patients-families/what-is-mental-illness

University, Q. (2018, July 17). Lobes of the brain. Retrieved from https://qbi.uq.edu.au/brain/brain-anatomy/lobes-brain

Riby, D. M., & Hancock, P. J. B. (2009). Do faces capture the ttention of individuals with Williams syndrome or autism? Evidence from tracking eye movements. Journal of Autism and Developmental Disorders. https://doi.org/10.1007/s10803-008-0641-z

Rizzolatti, G., & Sinigaglia, C. (2010). The functional role of the parieto-frontal mirror circuit: Interpretations and misinterpretations. Nature Reviews Neuroscience,11(4), 264-274. doi:10.1038/nrn2805

Salazar, F., Baird, G., Chandler, S., Tseng, E., O'sullivan, T., Howlin, P., ... Simonoff, E. (2015). Co-occurring Psychiatric Disorders in Preschool and Elementary School-Aged Children with Autism Spectrum Disorder. Journal of Autism and Developmental Disorders, 45(8), 2283–94. https://doi.org/10.1007/s10803-015-2361-5

Spezio, M. L., Adolphs, R., Hurley, R. S. E., & Piven, J. (2007). Abnormal use of facial information in high-functioning autism. Journal of Autism and Developmental Disorders. https://doi.org/10.1007/s10803-006-0232-9

Tantam, D. (2003). The challenge of adolescents and adults with Asperger syndrome. Child and Adolescent Psychiatric Clinics of North America, 12(1), 143–163. https://doi.org/10.1016/S1056-4993(02)00053-6

Made in the USA
Middletown, DE
21 March 2020

86998491R00113